5-MINUTE DEVOTIONS FOR TEENS

5-MINUTE DEVOTIONS FOR TEENS

A GUIDE TO GOD AND MENTAL HEALTH

LAURA L. SMITH

ZONDERKIDZ

5-Minute Devotions for Teens: A Guide to God and Mental Health

Copyright © 2022 by Laura L. Smith

Requests for information should be addressed to:

Zonderkidz, 3900 Sparks Dr. SE, Grand Rapids, Michigan 49546

ISBN 978-0-310-14308-6 (softcover)
ISBN 978-0-310-14310-9 (audio)
ISBN 978-0-310-14309-3 (ebook)

Library of Congress Cataloging-in-Publication Data on File

Printed in the United States of America

HB 05.20.2024

INTRODUCTION

Dear friend,

As a mom of four kids (two girls and two boys, ages 23, 20, 18, and 15), I've seen firsthand how anything and everything can come at a teenager. But I've also experienced firsthand the constant love of Jesus, who is there no matter what comes our way.

I've seen my kids get chosen for the play, the team, and the scholarship. I've also seen them get benched, betrayed, and turned down. I've experienced high highs and low lows with them. My kids and I have laughed, celebrated, and cried together throughout their teen years. I've walked with them through minor and not-so-minor mental health setbacks. I've seen Jesus show up time and time again to get them through, hold them up, remind them they're loved, open a new door, and work something bad for good. He'll do this for you too.

As I wrote these devotions, I kept all the things my kids have been through in mind, the things we've prayed about together, the ways God has shown up for them, the things I still pray they know down in their hearts.

Throughout the pages of this book, I've included tips from professionals on how to take care of your mental health. But I've also put the biblical truths that explain the "why" behind the suggestions on how to care for your mental health. For example, it's good for your mental health to get outside. This is God's perfect plan. He created all of nature. When you get out in nature, you feel God more, sense Him more clearly. It makes sense that being outside—closer to God and His creation—helps calm and refresh you.

Each devotion includes a prayer or a prompt. You'll find a notes section in the back of the book to record your prompt responses and thoughts.

I pray as you read this book, you'll become more equipped to take care of your mental health, now, in your teen years, and throughout your life. But even more so, I pray that you'll feel the sweet, deep love of Jesus for you. That you'll know He is for you, that He wants only good for you, that He'll fight for you, and that He'll never leave your side.

Love,

Laura L. Smith

For you created my inmost being; you knit
me together in my mother's womb.
I praise you because I am fearfully and wonderfully made.
PSALM 139:13–14

ARE YOU ARTSY? ATHLETIC? LOUD? QUIET? SERIOUS OR hilarious? Competitive or easygoing? Do you like to build things, cook, or go for hikes? No matter what you like or how you look, you are made fearfully and wonderfully by God. And that word "fearfully" doesn't mean "scary"—it means "to inspire awe," as in awesome.

The world (including social media) will try to tell you otherwise. That you don't measure up.

But let it sink in that the Creator of the universe, who is in charge of everything, intentionally sewed you together stitch by stitch before you were born. And all those special things about you—the shape of your eyebrows, the sound of your laugh, the things that make your brain tick, that you're curious about, that bring an uncontrollable smile to your face—God put all that in you, and He did it on purpose. God made you, and He made you awesome.

What makes you you? What do you love to do? What excites or calms you? In the notes section, sketch a picture of yourself or of something that symbolizes you. Thank God for making you exactly who you are. Write the words "wonderful" and "awesome" somewhere on the page to remind yourself how God created you.

DAY 2

*For ever since the world was created, people have seen the
earth and sky. Through everything God made, they can clearly
see his invisible qualities—his eternal power and divine
nature. So they have no excuse for not knowing God.*

ROMANS 1:20 NLT

WHEN WAS THE LAST TIME YOU WENT OUTSIDE? AND NOT just to stand at the bus stop or to walk from a building to a climate-controlled car. According to the American Psychological Association, getting outdoors can help improve your attention, lower your stress, put you in a better mood, and reduce your risk of mental health disorders such as anxiety and depression.[1]

This makes total sense. God created the earth and everything in it. Every tree, rock, creek, flower, frog, squirrel, and bug. Enjoying nature is good for your body, mind, and soul. The fresh air, the trickle of a stream or the crash of a wave, the song of a bird, the sweet scent of wildflowers, or the stunning colors of a sunset— they all reach somewhere inside you. Getting outdoors can calm your thoughts, inspire curiosity, and spark creativity. It can remind you of God's great power and love.

Go outside today. Walk a trail, climb a tree, sit by a stream, or spread out a blanket and gaze at the stars. Look around. Listen. Let yourself enjoy your surroundings. Take a moment to thank God for creating so many different and amazing things.

When Jesus spoke again to the people, he said, "I am the light of the world. Whoever follows me will never walk in darkness, but will have the light of life."

JOHN 8:12

YOU WILL HAVE DARK DAYS. DAYS WHEN A FRIEND BREAKS your trust and your feelings are hurt, and you have no idea what to say. Days when depression feels heavy, like it's weighing you down. Days when everything seems to be going wrong.

But there is good news. Jesus is light. He's brighter and lovelier than anything you can imagine and more powerful than any dark thing you're facing. Jesus promises that if you follow Him, you'll have the light of life. That might mean Jesus will give you the right words to speak to your friend or a safe place to go when things feel overwhelming. Or maybe He'll provide a surprise that cuts through your darkness like a fluffy kitten jumping on your lap or your mom making your favorite meal or a snow day. Sometimes Jesus lights up a way out of an unhealthy situation and toward a healthy one. Jesus offers you better and brighter and wants you to live in His wonderful light.

Walk into a dark room and turn on the light. Notice the difference it makes. Ask Jesus to light up your life, to add brightness to anywhere that's dark.

3

DAY 4

*Therefore, if anyone is in Christ, the new creation
has come: The old has gone, the new is here!*

2 CORINTHIANS 5:17

YOU KNOW THAT FIRST CHILLY DAY OF THE SEASON WHEN you pull out the sweatpants you haven't worn in months, because it's been too warm, only to realize they're way too short? You've grown and those sweats no longer fit you.

Living with Jesus also helps us grow—not our bodies, but our hearts and souls. In the process, there are some things that don't fit us well anymore—like friendships that are no longer healthy or habits that don't serve us well or a grudge against someone that's not worth holding on to. Jesus gives us the freedom to put all that old stuff behind us, to get rid of it and move into new things, better things, friendships and activities and emotions that fit us way better. Just like you can clean out your closet to get rid of clothes that no longer fit, you can clean out your life by pitching what you've spiritually outgrown. When you do, you'll find yourself as a new creation, better and freer than ever.

Take a few minutes to consider who you hang out with, the activities you do, your daily eating, sleeping, and viewing habits and see if there's anything that doesn't fit the life Jesus offers you. If so, take a step to pitch it—delete an app, unfollow the "friend" who always puts you down, throw away the food that hurts your stomach, et cetera.

You are to be holy to me because I, the LORD, am holy, and
I have set you apart from the nations to be my own.
LEVITICUS 20:26

SOMETIMES YOU WON'T GET PICKED. YOU WON'T GET selected for the team. You won't be put in the advanced class. You won't get a part in the play. You won't get called on even though your hand is raised high. You won't get invited to the party.

It happens to all of us. And it hurts. But even if someone else doesn't choose you, God does pick you. Always!

God calls you to be His daughter or son. God chooses you to love. He sets you apart, and not off to the side somewhere, but to be His very own—for an exciting, fulfilling life filled with love and acceptance. No matter who else does or doesn't choose you, God chooses you every day. He loves you for who you are. He sees you and He wants you on His team. God sets you in the highest places. He gives you the leading role. God wants to hear what you have to say, and He promises to be with you always.

Think of something coming up you hope you get chosen for (the starting lineup, the art show, a scholarship, etc.). Let God know what you're hoping for, but also thank Him for choosing you to be His blessed child. Ask God to remind you how special you are to Him (and to be able to hold on to that) whether you get chosen or not.

DAY 6

The night is nearly over; the day is almost here. So let us put
aside the deeds of darkness and put on the armor of light.

ROMANS 13:12

"EVERY MORNING WHEN YOU WAKE UP, NEW BABY NERVE cells have been born while you were sleeping that are there at your disposal to be used in tearing down toxic thoughts and rebuilding healthy thoughts," says neuroscientist Dr. Caroline Leaf.[2]

Isn't that so cool? Every day is a new opportunity to put aside dark thoughts, negative thoughts, hurtful thoughts, and to replace them with healthy, positive thoughts.

How do you do it? You can start by reading a list of five wonderful, true things about you and your life each morning. Maybe that could be "I'm stronger than I give myself credit for." Maybe it's a skill you're good at or a certain way you know you've been blessed. "Math comes easily to me." Or "God has given me a safe home." Do this before you turn on social media. Before you talk to someone who brings you down. Before you let negative self-talk tell you something bad about yourself. This shuts down dark thoughts and arms your thought life with light.

＊＊＊

Use the notes section and create the list you'll read each morning. Write out five awesome truths about yourself and/or your life— your gifts or talents, someone who cares about you, some positive circumstances you've been blessed with. I'll get you started:

1. God loves you endlessly, no matter what.

The LORD is close to the brokenhearted
and saves those who are crushed in spirit.

PSALM 34:18

HAVE YOU EVER FELT HEARTBROKEN? WHEN YOUR PET died? When the person you liked went with someone else to the dance? When someone you trusted let you down—big-time? When the thing you desperately looked forward to got canceled? Crummy things happen in this world. Sometimes crushing things.

But God promises to be close. He promises to save you.

God's not going to leave you. He wants to rescue you from the pain, the sadness, the shame, the disappointment, the fear, the hurt feelings, all of it. That doesn't stop bad things from happening, but it does change the way they affect you. Because God can comfort and heal you. He'll offer you joy and remind you that He created you for amazing things. God will protect you and help you move forward if you let Him. All you have to do is talk to God, ask for His help, trust that what He says is true. And He'll be right there, so very close, ready to save you.

Dear Jesus, thank You for being close to me even when I feel heartbroken. Thank You for saving me. I want all the comfort and joy You offer. Help me deepen my relationship with You, so I can fully feel Your love and protection. Amen.

DAY 8

For I am convinced that neither death nor life, neither angels nor demons, neither the present nor the future, nor any powers, neither height nor depth, nor anything else in all creation, will be able to separate us from the love of God that is in Christ Jesus our LORD.

ROMANS 8:38–39

GOD LOVES YOU! THIS ISN'T SOMETHING TO SHRUG YOUR shoulders at. The God of the universe, the One who created mammoth mountains and mighty oceans, giant elephants and cuddly koalas, juicy oranges, spicy peppers, unfathomable rainbows, and thumping heartbeats. That God created you. He loves you. And there's absolutely nothing, you can do or anyone else can do to change that.

You failed your test, quit the team, did something super embarrassing, made a mess of things, screamed at your best friend? God still loves you. Someone abused you or lied to you or ignored you or bullied you or told you horrible, awful things? God's heart breaks when you're treated poorly. God loves you. The Bible says nothing can separate you from God's love. As in not a single thing. Nothing. Live in His perfect love today. God loves you. No matter what.

Dear Jesus, it seems almost too good to be true. But it is true. You love me. Thank You for loving me always. For not letting anything come between Your love and me. Help me believe and hold on to Your perfect love. Amen.

"Have I not commanded you? Be strong and courageous.
Do not be afraid; do not be discouraged, for the LORD
your God will be with you wherever you go."
JOSHUA 1:9

DO YOU GET ANXIOUS IN CROWDS? ARE YOU AFRAID OF the dark? Of being alone? Maybe there's someone who threatens or intimidates you—a coach, or bully. Sometimes it's a certain place or incident that feels scary, or somewhere that reminds you of something bad in your past.

Do you remember the Cowardly Lion in *The Wizard of Oz*? He was afraid of everything and would do almost anything to get courage. But you don't have to fight off flying monkeys or follow the yellow brick road to get courage.

God says He'll be with you wherever you go, in every situation. God can be your courage. God says there's nothing to be afraid of because He's right by your side. He'll stand beside you when you feel threatened or nervous. God will hold you when your heart races or when your hands shake. God doesn't give you a gold badge to pin to your shirt. He gives you something better—strength, courage, and love in everything you're facing.

Make a list of what you're afraid of. It doesn't matter if it's truly terrifying or if it's something that may seem silly, like spiders—write them down. Then take a black marker and write over the entire list, "Do not be afraid! God is with me!"

9

Love is patient, love is kind.
1 CORINTHIANS 13:4

ARE YOU PATIENT WITH YOURSELF? GOD IS.

Yes, He wants you to use the talents He's given you to seize the day and fully embrace the incredible life He has in store for you. But God isn't rushing you or timing you on how much you get done or how quickly you swim your laps or unload the dishwasher. He wants you to go, live, experience. But God is patient with you in the process.

Are you kind to yourself? God is.

Do you look in the mirror and think kind thoughts? Do you forgive yourself quickly if you said the wrong thing or didn't say anything or fell on your face? Do you give yourself time to collect your thoughts before you go again? Do you allow yourself to draw or journal or take a long, relaxing shower or use your imagination? God is so kind to you. He thinks the very best things about you, has forgiven any mistake you made or will make, urges you to rest and breathe and process, and absolutely loves it when you practice self-care.

God's love is patient and kind. Try being more patient and kind with yourself.

Dear Jesus, thank You for Your kindness. Thank You for Your patience with me. Help me feel and understand how truly kind and patient You are. Help me be patient and kind with myself today. Amen.

Jesus wept.
JOHN 11:35

DID YOU KNOW JESUS CRIED?

Jesus' friend Lazarus died. There was a big group of people all crying and mourning the loss of this man. Jesus was God. He could do anything. In fact, a few minutes after He wept, Jesus brought Lazarus back to life. Jesus knew He was going to do that, knew He was totally capable of raising Lazarus, but Jesus was still sad, and He allowed Himself to feel His feelings.

Jesus wants you to feel your feelings too. Not just hold them inside or push them away or numb them with distractions. If you're sad today, allow yourself to cry. If you're scared about something, confide in someone what you're worried about. If you're happy, crank the tunes and sing at the top of your lungs. Tell somebody what made you joyful. If you're confused, ask questions that might help you figure out what's going on. Jesus came down to earth to show us how to best live this life. If Jesus cried, that means it's okay for you to feel your feelings too.

How are you feeling today? In the notes section, journal about your mood and why you feel that way. Then share your feelings with someone you trust—not online, not over text, but face-to-face with a real person (or at least via a video chat).

*Do you not know that your bodies are temples of the Holy
Spirit, who is in you, whom you have received from God?*

1 CORINTHIANS 6:19

GOD CREATED YOUR BODY. THEREFORE, GOD WANTS YOU to take care of your body. That can mean all kinds of things—eating healthy foods, getting enough sleep, avoiding things that will cause harm to your body (like smoking or alcohol). It also means using your body in an honorable way—to do kind, productive things, to avoid sex outside of marriage or any kind of inappropriate behavior with your body.

Exercise is something specific you can do to honor God with your body. Exercise releases feel-good chemicals in your brain called endorphins. These endorphins help reduce mental health struggles like anxiety and depression and in general boost your mood. Even if you're tired or it feels like a lot of effort, a simple fifteen-minute walk can boost your mood. Find a kind of exercise you enjoy—doing push-ups or jumping jacks during a commercial break, dancing to your favorite song, walking your dog, or going on a bike ride with a friend. Get moving today—both to thank God for making your body and to increase your happiness.

*Dear Jesus, thank You for creating my body. For a heart that beats
and a mind that thinks. Please help me be aware of how important
it is to care for this body. Thank You for creating endorphins that
boost my mood and movement that creates endorphins. Amen.*

After he had dismissed them, he went up on a mountainside
by himself to pray. Later that night, he was there alone.
MATTHEW 14:23

LIFE CAN BE LOUD. FROM THE MOMENT YOUR ALARM wakes you up, your ears are filled with noise. The sound of people talking and of other students in the halls. The noise of TV, podcasts, music, texts, and the videos you watch. It's not all bad. Some of it is great—like the beat of your favorite song or the voice of someone you trust. But all that noise all the time can be overwhelming to your brain, your heart, and your soul.

Jesus often went off by Himself to be quiet. Not to isolate Himself, but just to take a break from all the noise. To talk to God. To sort His thoughts. Jesus knew how to take care of Himself and wants you to take care of yourself too. Taking a few minutes to be quiet can improve your concentration and focus, calm your racing thoughts, stimulate brain growth and creativity, and help you sleep better. [3]

Take five minutes of silence. Go somewhere quiet. Set an alarm on your phone and turn off all your other notifications. Talk to God about anything that's on your mind and let your thoughts s-l-o-w down.

The LORD makes firm the steps of the one who delights in him; though he may stumble, he will not fall, for the LORD upholds him with his hand.

PSALM 37:23-24

IS YOUR ROOM SO MESSY IT WILL TAKE FOREVER TO clean? Do you have so much homework you'll never get through it? Do you have so many things to get done you have no clue how you'll make them all happen?

When you feel overwhelmed, it's best to take one thing at a time. First, put away your clean shirts, and then maybe make your bed. Or choose one assignment to start with. When you're finished with it, you can do one more. Taking your to-dos in chunks makes them less stressful and more manageable. But where should you start?

God promises to make your steps firm, and to hold your hand so you won't fall along the way. If you ask God, He'll help you figure out where to start. And then what to do after that and after that. If you mess up along the way, it's okay. God will help you get back on track and get going again.

Dear God, thank You so much for helping me with all the steps in my life. Please show me where to start, how to organize my time, and not get too overwhelmed in the process. I'm so grateful You're here with me to hold my hand. Amen.

*The tempter came to him and said, "If you are the Son
of God, tell these stones to become bread."
Jesus answered, "It is written: 'Man shall not live on bread alone,
but on every word that comes from the mouth of God.'"*

MATTHEW 4:3-4

JESUS WENT TO THE WILDERNESS TO FAST, PRAY, AND BE
with God. The devil knew Jesus was hungry and tried to get Jesus
to turn rocks into food. Jesus could have done that. No problem.
But He did not want to listen to the devil. He wanted to trust God.
So what did Jesus do?

Jesus quoted Scripture to Satan. Jesus chose a specific verse
that says what we really need to live on is God's Word—the Bible.
It's full of truth about who God is and how He loves you. The more
often you read the Bible, the better you know it, and the better
you'll be able to stand up to anything the enemy throws your way.
You'll also feel satisfied, not just by fresh bread or tasty snacks, but
by the very Word of God. Satan tried tempting Jesus three times.
All three times Jesus spoke words from the Bible as a defense. You
know what happened next? The devil went away (Matthew 4:11).

Read your Bible today. Not just a verse or two, but maybe a whole
chapter. Not sure where to start? The book of John is a perfect
starting place. The Psalms make super prayers. And the letters to
the early church (like Romans, Ephesians, and Galatians) all give
great advice on what it's like to have a relationship with Jesus.

"For where two or three gather in my name, there am I with them."

MATTHEW 18:20

EVER HAVE A HARD TIME LIVING HOW YOU KNOW GOD wants you to live? When your classmates talk about the weird substitute teacher, it's hard not to chime in. When your friends want to go somewhere your parents have said you can't go, it's tricky to say, "Let's get ice cream instead." But if you have a friend (or two) who loves Jesus, who wants to honor God with their actions, it gets a lot easier. Together, you and your friend can say something nice about the sub or change the subject when someone talks badly about them. When you suggest ice cream, your friend can back you up. This doesn't mean God isn't with you when you're alone. He's with you always.

Don't have friends like this? Pay attention. I bet you'll notice someone on your team or in class who chooses good words and good works. Get to know them. Ask them to be your partner on a project or sit next to them at the game. Life's easier when you have someone who stands up for what you believe in with you.

Name a friend who helps you stay close to God. If you don't have friends like this, list some people you think might know God, some kids who make good decisions. Thank God for your Christian friends or ask Him to help you find some. Then ask God to help you stand strong together.

Then Samuel took a stone and set it up between Mizpah and Shen.
He named it Ebenezer, saying, "Thus far the LORD has helped us."

1 SAMUEL 7:12

IS THERE A TIME GOD HELPED YOU? A TIME YOU REMEM-
ber feeling God with you? Have you ever prayed for something, and
God answered that prayer? Or maybe there was a special time at
camp or church or during worship when you really felt God's love.

How often do you thank God for that thing? When times
are hard or God feels far away, do you recall that special God
moment—or dwell on the problem in front of you?

God loves you. So much. And He will fight for you, stand by
you, hold you, show you the way, and love you completely over and
over again. When God does these things, it's important to take
notice. Maybe jot it down in your journal or snap a photo of the
campfire where you felt God's presence. The prophet Samuel didn't
have a journal or a phone, so he picked up a stone, set it up, and
named it Ebenezer (which means "remember") so he and the whole
Jewish nation could remember how God saved them one day.

Do you have a journal page, photo, ticket, or rock that reminds you
of something God did for you or a special time you've felt God's
love? The next time you're struggling, go back to your "Ebenezer
stone," and remember how good, loving, and personal God is—
that He's on your side.

DAY 18

But those who hope in the LORD will renew their strength.
They will soar on wings like eagles; they will run and
not grow weary, they will walk and not be faint.

ISAIAH 40:31

SOME DAYS YOU'LL FEEL EXHAUSTED. IT COULD BE because you stayed up doing homework, you had a late game or practice, you had a lot on your mind and couldn't fall asleep, you're run-down or not feeling well, or maybe all of the above happened several days in a row.

Whew! It's hard to concentrate and keep going when you feel like this. The best thing to do when you're exhausted is get some sleep. But it's also important to remember that God promises to renew you—just like a power nap.

If you put your hope in God, He'll help you soar during the important times, even when you feel like you can barely crawl. That doesn't mean you won't ever feel tired or that you should stay up extremely late. It means when you trust in God, He will give you extra energy you didn't have on your own, to do the things He calls you to do.

If your bedtime's been late, try to figure out how to go to bed earlier this week. And ask God to give you the energy you need to do the important stuff. Write out today's verse and put it where you'll see it in the morning (maybe on the bathroom mirror) to remind you that God offers you energy and strength each day.

For God so loved the world that he gave his one and only Son, that
whoever believes in him shall not perish but have eternal life.

JOHN 3:16

GOD LOVES YOU. HE DOES. EVEN WHEN IT FEELS LIKE NO one understands you, like no one else loves you, like no one else cares, or like God is a million miles away. God loves you.

How can you know for sure? Because God sent His Son, Jesus, down to earth to become a person, so He would know exactly what it was like to be stressed, excited, hurt, happy, sad, nervous, even bullied, hungry, and tired. God wanted to understand everything about you. You're that important to God!

And then God allowed His perfect Son to die on the cross and take the punishment for anything wrong you've ever done or ever will do, so that you could be free and forgiven. Wow! Not because you did something amazing, but because God would do anything for you, give up anything for you, even die for you. So, if you're wondering if anyone cares, if anyone understands, know down to your core that God loves you. He wants only the best for you. And God would do anything; in fact, He did everything, so that He can be with you forever.

Think of someone you love. It could be your pet, a friend, or a family member. Would you give up everything for them? God did that for you. Thank God for giving up the thing that was most valuable to Him for you, for loving you that much.

He said: "The LORD is my rock, my fortress and my
deliverer; my God is my rock, in whom I take refuge."

2 SAMUEL 22:2-3

YOU MEASURE HOW TALL YOU ARE WITH A MEASURING stick. You measure how hard minerals are with a system called the Mohs' scale. The hardest mineral is a diamond. It is a ten out of ten on the Mohs' scale. It's so hard that the only thing that can cut a diamond is another diamond! Why is it important how hard a rock is? Because the harder the rock, the more it resists scratching. The hardest rocks can make it through storms, travel great distances, endure intense heat, and they're the best at polishing other rocks.

The LORD is your rock—the hardest kind of all, stronger than a diamond, higher than a ten on the Mohs' scale! Why is that important? Because it means God can help polish you into the best version of yourself. No one else can. God can protect you from being scratched. God can help you through the storms of life, travel great distances with you, and help you stand strong no matter how much heat you're in. God is the ultimate Rock. Cling to His strength today!

Go for a walk and gather some small rocks. Try scratching them against each other. Whichever one is the strongest will make the most marks on the others and have the fewest on it. Put the strongest rock in your pocket or backpack as a reminder of God's strength in your life.

Rejoice always, pray continually, give thanks in all
circumstances; for this is God's will for you in Christ Jesus.
1 THESSALONIANS 5:16–18

ON ANY GIVEN DAY THINGS COULD BE AWESOME OR awful. You may get a fever or lose a notebook or find ten dollars on the ground. You might forget your lunch or have warm chocolate chip cookies waiting for you when you get home. But no matter what is going on in your life, God is good, and He loves you.

Because God loves you so much, He is always doing good things for you. Sometimes it takes intentionality to focus on those things instead of the bad things. But the good things are there. You can be grateful for a stunning sunrise, cozy covers, or a ride to practice.

If you're having the best or worst day you can thank God for something, anything—your favorite sweatshirt, spaghetti for dinner, the smell of rain. When you are grateful it helps you remember how good God is, how much He loves you, that He is always there and doing good things for you. Always.

In the notes section write, "Dear Jesus, I am thankful for . . ." List five things you are thankful for.

1. I'm also so thankful for Your love and goodness for me. Amen.

*You alone are the LORD. You made the heavens, even the
highest heavens, and all their starry host, the earth and all
that is on it, the seas and all that is in them. You give life to
everything, and the multitudes of heaven worship you.*

NEHEMIAH 9:6

THE CLOSEST STAR TO THE EARTH IS THE SUN. IT'S 93 MIL-
lion miles away. The next closest stars (Alpha Centauri A and B)
are 4.35 light years away from us. And yet the entire sky is dotted
with the bright, beautiful lights of the stars God created.

The oceans cover more than 70 percent of the earth! All that
salt water would fill 352,670,000,000,000,000,000 gallon-sized
milk containers. God made every drop of it.

God made every tree, lake, mountain, and living thing. And He
decided to make you. It's hard to get our brains around how amazing
God is, how all-encompassing He is. If God can make all the stars
and planets, including the Earth, and its oceans, and everything on
it, He can do anything. He can help you in your hardest times. He
can show you a safe way out of a struggle. He can heal your pain. He
is more capable than you can imagine, and He's on your side.

What is overwhelming you today? Consider the facts above about
stars and oceans. Thank God for being bigger than the solar
system and deeper than the ocean. Ask Him to use His endless
power, intellect, creativity, and resourcefulness to help you
through your struggle.

*And we know that in all things God works for the good of those
who love him, who have been called according to his purpose.*

ROMANS 8:28

DID YOUR GAME GET RAINED OUT? MAYBE GOD WILL GIVE
you some needed rest with those unexpected free hours. Nervous
about moving? Your future best friend might be waiting for you
at your new school. Homework seems overwhelming? God could
use the very thing you learn in biology to help you find a cure for
a disease someday.

God doesn't make bad things. He's 100 percent good and can
only do good. But God can take the bad things and use them for
your good.

God can take an argument with a family member and use it as
a way for you both to actually understand each other better. God
can take the trip to the grocery with your mom that you really don't
want to go on as a way to provide you with the exact thing you need
for your project that you forgot you needed.

Whatever you're facing today—something at home, your
health, whatever it is—God can work good through these things,
even the hard ones.

*Dear Jesus, can You please help? Can You calm my emotions and
help me be mindful of the fact that I can trust You to turn this
bad thing into something good? Please turn it into good, LORD.
Thank You! Amen.*

DAY 24

"Do not grieve, for the joy of the LORD is your strength."

NEHEMIAH 8:10

DO YOU LOVE THE SOUND OF A TRAIN, THE SMELL OF vanilla, the thrill of a roller coaster, camping, hiking, fishing, or anything that's in the woods?

Or maybe God created you to thrive in the energy at a concert, adore walking barefoot, and love spicy food—the hotter the better. God made everybody one of a kind. When He created you, He made you able to experience joy through all kinds of specific things.

What place makes you feel good when you're there? What person makes you smile? What food delights you? What kind of music makes you sing along? Seek these things today. If your best friend fills you up, be intentional about getting together with them. If playing Frisbee always feels fun, grab a disc and toss it with a friend or your dog. If baking calms your anxious feelings, whip up a batch of fudgy brownies. God offers us joy. The joy of knowing Him. The joy of being loved by Him. And the joy of a world full of things He put specifically in your life for you.

Thank You, Jesus, for all the wonderful things You put in this world that bring me joy! Please help me seek these things and remember they are all gifts from You. Amen.

We demolish arguments and every pretension that sets
itself up against the knowledge of God, and we take
captive every thought to make it obedient to Christ.

2 CORINTHIANS 10:5

HUMANS HAVE OVER SIX THOUSAND THOUGHTS EACH DAY.
Some are important, like remembering an equation for a test. Some
thoughts are harmful, like if someone walks past without saying
"hi" or doesn't text back and you think: Maybe they don't like me.
Maybe I'm unlikeable. Your thoughts might even spin further:
Fine, if they're going to be like that, I'll ignore them too.

But maybe that person didn't see your text or you. Or maybe
they're going through something difficult, or their phone was
dead. When your thoughts spiral to negative, painful, or hurtful
thoughts toward yourself or others, you can stop those spirals by
grabbing the thought and holding it up to what Jesus says is true.

Jesus says He loves you, that you're holy, that you're made in
His image. So, you aren't unlikeable. You're loveable. And Jesus
tells us to love one another, so doing something unkind to someone else also isn't listening to what Jesus says. When you find
yourself thinking negative thoughts, pause, grab a hold of that
thought, and ask Jesus what He says.

Journal any negative thoughts about yourself or others you had
today. One by one, ask Jesus if they're true. How do your thoughts
hold up?

Because of the LORD's great love we are not consumed,
for his compassions never fail. They are new every
morning; great is your faithfulness.

LAMENTATIONS 3:22-23

TODAY IS A BRAND-NEW DAY FULL OF POSSIBILITIES AND potential. The sun rose in the sky this morning and your lungs are breathing fresh air. Wherever you're going today, you have a chance to have a meaningful chat with a friend or meet a new one. You have the opportunity to make someone else smile or do something good for yourself. You have the chance to try or learn something new. Whatever happened yesterday is over. Don't let the stress from missing the shot at practice or that hurtful thing someone said yesterday overwhelm you today. You can learn from it. You can grow from it. You can also move on from it.

So what would you like to do today? Go for a bike ride? Improve your grade in English? Practice dribbling? Bake? Call your grandma? Write a song? God is with you on this day, loving you and cheering for you in all that you're experiencing. God is excited to see what adventures you'll go on and how you'll live this amazing gift of twenty-four hours to its fullest.

If you could do anything today, what would it be? Ask God what He thinks is the best use of your time today. Praise Him for the opportunities that await you and seize them when they come your way.

"Don't be afraid, I've redeemed you. I've called your name. You're mine.
When you're in over your head, I'll be there with you.
When you're in rough waters, you will not go down.
When you're between a rock and a hard place, it won't be a dead end—"

ISAIAH 43:1-2 MSG

THERE ARE DAYS WHEN YOU'LL FEEL LIKE YOU'RE IN OVER your head, like you're drowning or stuck. But God says, "Don't be afraid." Why? Because you're His. The God of the universe, who makes everything—from bolts of electricity flashing through the sky to tiny lightning bugs who glow in the dark—says you belong to Him. He says He loves you so much He calls you by name—He knows your name, knows exactly who you are, everything about you, and calls out to you, because He wants to be with you, to show you His love, to care for you.

God won't let you go down, no matter how far or fast it feels like you're falling. You just have to reach out to Him. He'll catch you in His arms and save you. You see, if God promises to be with you and rescue you no matter what (and He does), you don't have anything to be afraid of.

Dear Jesus, thank You for keeping me afloat, for guiding me out of dead-end situations. Thank You for knowing me and calling me Yours, for loving me so much. I reach out to You today and accept Your help. Please hold me up and show me where to go. Amen.

"I will give you a new heart and put a new spirit in you; I will remove from you your heart of stone and give you a heart of flesh."

EZEKIEL 36:26

EVER SAID SOMETHING NASTY AND WISHED YOU COULD take it back? Ever told your parents that you did your chores, sent that email, or studied for that test, even though you hadn't . . . yet? Ever been jealous of someone else's clothes or curfew or car? Ever lost your temper? Stomped out of the room? Slammed a door? Said something hurtful on purpose?

We are human. And we mess up. Thankfully, Jesus doesn't expect us to be perfect. In fact, He loves us for exactly who we are, for exactly who He made us to be. That's why God is always there for us, always guiding us, helping us to learn from our mistakes, giving us patience to not get so frustrated, peace to not get so angry, contentment in what we have, so we don't wish for what we don't have. If we ask Him for help, God will take out the bad stuff that bogs down our thoughts and actions and replace it with a more caring, loving heart.

Dear God, I hand over to You all the ways I've messed up. Please forgive me. Please help me do better next time; please remove my anger and bitterness and change my heart. Amen.

Now take a deep breath, a sigh of relief, knowing you have been completely forgiven. God is on your side.

*When the angel of the LORD appeared to Gideon, he
said, "The LORD is with you, mighty warrior."*
JUDGES 6:12

WHO DO YOU THINK OF WHEN YOU HEAR "MIGHTY WARRIOR"?
Black Panther taking down the bad guy to save his nation? Rosa
Parks for not giving up her seat on the bus? They were both pretty
mighty. But so are you! It's a weird thing to call yourself, but you are
a mighty warrior! You may not have a sword, shield, or lightsaber,
but you have something way more powerful. You have God.

What battles are you fighting today? Is there someone who
gets picked on in the cafeteria? You are a mighty warrior. You can
stand up to the bully, stand up for that person. Is there an athlete
on your team who is always last when you're running laps? You are
a mighty warrior. You can drop back and run alongside them, just
like a hero would go back in the fire to save someone. Is there something you're fighting—anxiety, depression, asthma—something
that makes you feel weak, like maybe you just can't do it today?
You are a mighty warrior! God has empowered you to fight your
battles and He's got your back every step of the way.

Picture yourself as a mighty warrior. Add in your "armor" or
"weapons" to fight your personal battles. And then picture God
next to you, the most powerful warrior of all. Whisper a prayer
asking Him for strength in all your battles today.

DAY 30

THE NEWEST PHONE, GAME SYSTEM, OR SOCIAL MEDIA app. The cool new place to hang out. The song everyone knows the words to. The show everyone is binge-watching.

There's so much to keep up with in our world. There's pressure to be in the know about all the things. And as soon as you catch up on one thing, you might feel behind on something else. Most people around you will do whatever is considered cool or fun in the moment, just because everyone else is. But God gave you a brain to decide for yourself. You get to choose how you spend your time and money, what you watch, say, play, wear, and listen to.

Sometimes the things everyone else seems hooked on are great—that song or account is really encouraging. But not always. Sometimes the lyrics are hateful, or the plotline is nasty, or the trend or game is inappropriate. God offers better. He offers good things, things that encourage you, that fill you with light and love. His will is pleasing. His will is good.

Dear Jesus, thank You for giving me a brain and the ability to make decisions for myself. Please help me not cave to what everyone else is doing but to choose to fill myself with things that are good and pleasing to You. Amen.

He [Elijah] came to a broom bush, sat down under it and
prayed that he might die. "I have had enough, LORD," he
said. "Take my life; I am no better than my ancestors."
Then he lay down under the bush and fell asleep.
All at once an angel touched him and said, "Get up and
eat." He looked around, and there by his head was some
bread baked over hot coals, and a jar of water.

1 KINGS 19:4-6

THE FAMOUS PROPHET ELIJAH SUFFERED FROM DEPRESSION.
Your good and loving God saw Elijah in his struggle and took care of
him. God didn't tell Elijah to blow it off or put on a happy face. God
let Elijah rest, made sure he had a warm meal and that he hydrated.

The Bible doesn't sugarcoat Elijah's situation. God had this
part of Elijah's story stay in the Bible so you could know that sometimes people struggle with their mental health. And that's okay.
God sees you in these struggles and loves you. If you're feeling
a little off or stuck in a rut or feeling the full weight of depression, God wants to take care of you. Sometimes God's care might
include a nap and a snack, a great counselor to help you process
your thoughts and life, or a friend who brings you treats, asks the
perfect questions, or is an incredible listener. God sees your pain
and struggle. He'll take care of you.

Assess your mental health today. Thank God for seeing you right
where you are and ask Him for help.

DAY 32

For we are God's handiwork, created in Christ Jesus to do
good works, which God prepared in advance for us to do.
EPHESIANS 2:10

ALL OF US ARE CREATIVE IN SOME WAY OR ANOTHER. What do you like to make? Do you write songs? Do you love drawing? Are you handy, able to fix a motor or carve things out of wood? Or techy, able to design cool graphics or code?

Think of the things you make, how much effort and care you put into them, how much time you spend making them, how good it feels when you've completed your creation. That's how God feels about you. You are His handiwork. Not His sketch or doodle but the thing He spent time on, the thing He took special care creating. Do you prefer a specific cupcake frosting technique or adding beats to electronic music? Do you use special tools to take care of the finest details? That's how God created you—with all the flourishes and features carefully tended to. Not only did He design you specifically to be as fantastic and unique as you are, but God made you exactly how you are so you'd be capable of doing amazing things for Him and His kingdom.

Create something today—a poster, a card, a video, tacos—and as you make it, thank God for making you. As you think through the process, look it over and add finishing touches. Thank God for putting so much attention into creating you.

"And who knows but that you have come to your
royal position for such a time as this?"
ESTHER 4:14

YOU MAY NOT KNOW WHY YOU'RE IN THAT CLASS, WHY you have that assigned seat, why you live in your neighborhood, or why you ride your bus. But God does.

Queen Esther was an orphan. Her entire family had been forced to leave the land they came from. And yet she was chosen as queen. Esther didn't necessarily want to be queen. It was tense and sometimes terrifying living in the same castle as the angry, selfish, and cruel king. But God put orphaned, exiled Esther in that palace at that time for a specific reason. God's people, the Jews, were about to be killed, but when Esther got the courage to tell the king what was going on, and ask for him to spare her people, her entire nation was saved. Wow!

It may seem random sometimes where you've ended up. Sometimes it even feels unfair or like a punishment. But God put you where you are for a reason. He might ask you to speak up or lend a hand or be brave, but God picked you specifically to make a difference right where you are.

Is there a place you have to go, a person you have to sit by that has you asking, "Why?" Direct your question to God. "Why, God, am I here? How can You use me? What do You have planned for me in this place?" Then trust Him to do something spectacular.

He [Jesus] took Peter, James and John along with him, and he began to be deeply distressed and troubled. "My soul is overwhelmed with sorrow . . ."

MARK 14:33–34

YUP, YOU READ THAT RIGHT. JESUS WAS DISTRESSED, TROUBLED, and overwhelmed. Jesus came down to earth from heaven to become fully human while remaining fully God. Jesus wanted to know what it felt like to laugh and cry, to be hurt and scared and excited. He wanted to know so He could love you well when you experience these things.

When Jesus was at His lowest low, He did two things:

1. He brought His best friends with Him. The people He knew could help Him through hard times.
2. He prayed. In the very next verse, that's what Jesus did: "He fell to the ground and prayed" (Mark 14:35).

Jesus did these things to show you how to deal with your lowest lows. You don't have to go through the hard stuff alone. Surround yourself with people who care about you, whom you can trust. And talk to God.

Dear Jesus, thank You for coming to earth and experiencing the emotions I feel. Please give me people I can count on. Thank You for the people who love me well. Thank You for Your love. Please help me through this hard time. Amen.

They hid from the LORD God among the trees of the garden.
But the LORD God called to the man, "Where are you?"

GENESIS 3:8–9

AT THE BEGINNING OF HUMANKIND, AN EVIL SERPENT tricked Adam and Eve into eating fruit from the only tree God told them they shouldn't eat from. After eating the fruit, Adam and Eve ran and hid from God.

Even after they'd messed up, even after they'd disobeyed God, even when they ran away from Him, God still wanted to be with Adam and Eve. "Where are you?" He called.

No matter how much you've messed up. No matter what you said or did. No matter if you disobeyed your teacher, pastor, parents, or even God, God still wants to be with you. He loves you so much. He never wants you to be alone or feel like you have to hide anything from Him. God already knows everything you've done and how you feel about it, but Jesus died on the cross to erase all your mistakes. If you're trying to hide anything from God, even yourself, God is calling you. Not to punish you, but to love you, protect you, listen to you, get you back on track, and offer you His amazing grace.

Dear Jesus, thank You for wanting to be with me. For loving me even when I've messed up. Because of Your grace it's safe to let You know everything. Please help me overcome any fear I may have of being "found out" and instead let You love me. Amen.

The LORD watches over you—the LORD is your shade at your right hand;
the sun will not harm you by day, nor the moon by night. The LORD
will keep you from all harm—he will watch over your life. The LORD
will watch over your coming and going both now and forevermore.

PSALM 121:5-8

HAVE YOU EVER BEEN SO FRIGHTENED THAT YOU JUST can't shake the feeling of fear? Your brain knows you shouldn't be afraid of that thing. But it seems to have forgotten to tell the rest of you.

Wouldn't it be great to have a bodyguard walking, sitting, or riding next to you wherever you went? You do. God is your own personal bodyguard watching over you, protecting you. He's there beside you during the hours the sun is shining. He's there beside you during the hours the moon glows in the sky. He's there even when it's so cloudy or foggy that you can't see the sun or moon. God is there beside you everywhere you come and go. When fear creeps in, remember you are protected by the most incredibly powerful watchman—God.

Write out the verse above on a note card or in the notes section and put it somewhere you can pull out on nights you're feeling scared or mornings when you're facing something that frightens you. Read it and be reminded that God protects you today and always.

*[The LORD] is able to do immeasurably more than all we ask or
imagine, according to his power that is at work within us.*

EPHESIANS 3:20

WHAT IS YOUR DREAM? IF YOU COULD DO ANYTHING, ANY-
where, with anyone ten years from now, what would it be?

God plants all kinds of dreams in people's hearts. He gives you
things you're passionate about, things you're good at, things that
make you feel like you're at home, like you can be yourself, like
you're thriving. And then, because He's God, He gives you opportunities to make these dreams a reality.

That doesn't mean God will give you a million dollars if you
want it. But it does mean if you've always loved little kids, God
probably has something in store for you—maybe make you into a
teacher or coach. If listening to, writing, and playing music soothes
you and at the same time makes you feel more alive, God probably
has something with music in your future. Maybe you'll tour the
world playing the guitar in front of giant crowds. Maybe you'll be
a songwriter or a worship leader. The possibilities are endless. God
can do more than you could ever ask or imagine in your life.

*Dear Jesus, thank You for the dreams You put in my heart.
Please show me how to step into the amazing future You have
in store for me and to trust that You can do more than I can ask
or imagine. Amen.*

DAY 38

You are a hiding place for me; you preserve me from trouble; you surround me with shouts of deliverance.

PSALM 32:7 ESV

DO YOU HAVE A HIDING PLACE? A PLACE YOU GO WHEN everything feels like too much and you need to be by yourself? Maybe it's not an actual "place," but listening to music, drawing, or shooting hoops helps you process. It's a place that feels safe and separate from everything else. Maybe you go there when you're anxious or angry or when you don't want anyone to see your tears. It's a place where you can catch your breath, organize your thoughts, or have a good long cry.

There are times we can't get to our hiding places. Sometimes our secret spaces can't give us all the comfort we need. But God is the perfect refuge. When no one else understands, He does. When no one else is listening, He wants to hear. When you're concerned others will judge you or blame you, God will love you. Whenever you feel like you need your space, that you need time alone, go to God. He's waiting there just for you.

Where do you go when you need to be alone? Put a reminder there that God is your perfect safe place. When you feel overwhelmed, go to or visualize that space and picture God there waiting to comfort you. Thank Him for being your ultimate hiding place.

Give thanks to the LORD, for he is good; his love endures forever.
1 CHRONICLES 16:34

THE BIBLE TELLS US TO GIVE THANKS TO GOD, BUT IT'S not just for God's sake. (Sure, He likes to hear a thank-you now and then. Who doesn't?) It's actually for your good.

Mental health professionals agree that practicing gratitude makes people happier. Gratitude also has lasting positive effects on the human brain.

How does practicing gratitude work? It's simply taking a moment to thank God for something. You can say it out loud, think it in your head, or write it down, maybe in your journal. You can thank God for who He is, for something He's done for you in the past, or something He's doing right now, like the adorable card your grandma sent, a sweet refreshing slushie on a hot summer day, or your pet coming to meet you when you walk in the door. Being thankful flips a switch in your brain. You have to stop worrying because your brain is focusing on the good thing instead of anything bad you're experiencing or worried about. Ready to be happier? Start giving thanks to God. He's so very good. And His love endures forever.

In the notes section, write down at least five things you're grateful for.

DAY 40

Then Jesus said, "Let's go off by ourselves to a quiet place and rest awhile." He said this because there were so many people coming and going that Jesus and his apostles didn't even have time to eat.

MARK 6:31 NLT

WHEN WAS THE LAST TIME YOU HAD A HEALTHY MEAL? Turned off your phone? Got some exercise? Got a good night's sleep? Went outside? Are you avoiding foods you're allergic to or are bad for you? When you neglect your body, all kinds of things can go wrong. Sure, it can affect your physical health, but also your mood, mental health, even your relationships—including your relationship with God.

Taking care of your body should be a priority. It was for Jesus. He and His disciples had been working hard. They were tired and hungry. Jesus realized this and suggested they all take some time to rest and get a meal. Jesus knew His disciples would suffer if they didn't take care of their bodies. He knows this about you too. Taking care of your spiritual health and mental health are super important, but if you don't take care of your physical health, the other two could suffer. God made your body. Shouldn't you do your best to care for it?

Take a moment to assess your physical self. How many hours of sleep did you get last week? Are you eating a balanced diet? Do you exercise regularly? Set some goals for exercising self-care for your body this week and try to stick to them. Ask God for guidance and perseverance.

No temptation has overtaken you except what is common to mankind. And God is faithful; he will not let you be tempted beyond what you can bear. But when you are tempted, he will also provide a way out so that you can endure it.

1 CORINTHIANS 10:13

TEMPTATIONS ARE REAL AND THEY HIT US EVERY SINGLE day. Today you might be tempted to yell at your sister because she takes so long in the bathroom. You might be tempted to vape or drink or do something else with your body that you know isn't healthy. You might be tempted to watch a show or check out a website that you know you shouldn't when no one else is around. Maybe your temptations today will be different. But you will be tempted. The good news is God is faithful.

When temptations come up, no matter how good they look, no matter how hard it might feel to say no, God will provide a way out for you, a way for you to avoid making the wrong choice. The Bible also says God won't let you be tempted more than you can bear. That means God has already given you the ability to turn away from everything you're tempted by. You can handle it. Ask for God's help. He'll show you a way out.

Is there anything that tempts you regularly? Ask God for the right words, the right ideas, another path, or another way. Ask God to make it clear what you're supposed to do in the moment of temptation. Then thank Him for being so faithful.

DAY 42

"My grace is all you need. My power works best in weakness."
2 CORINTHIANS 12:9 NLT

SOMETIMES IT ALL FEELS LIKE TOO MUCH. WAY TOO MUCH.
Like you'll never be able to understand your assignment, make it
to all the practices, find time to clean your room, be patient with
your little brother, or find your phone charger. There doesn't feel
like enough of you to go around.

This is where God likes to show off. The Bible says you don't
have to be perfect. In fact, you can't be. But God is. And in all
the places you feel you're not fast enough, smart enough, strong
enough, creative enough, or like you don't have the time, resources,
or energy to do things how you'd hope, Jesus steps in and fills all
the cracks with His grace. He might free up an hour of time or
give you more patience than you knew you had. God might have
someone else do a chore for you, give you a ride, or find the thing
you've misplaced. And even when things still don't go as planned,
Jesus offers grace. He says, "It's okay. You don't have to be all the
things for all the people. Exhale. Know that you are fully loved by
Me. No matter what."

Where do you feel like you don't have enough today? Post the
words, "My grace is all you need." Somewhere you'll see it
throughout the week (as your screen saver, on a sticky note on
your mirror, inside your locker, etc.).

And I pray that you, being rooted and established in love, may have power, together with all the LORD's holy people, to grasp how wide and long and high and deep is the love of Christ, and to know this love that surpasses knowledge—that you may be filled to the measure of all the fullness of God.

EPHESIANS 3:17–19

IN THE RAINY SEASON, THE AMAZON RIVER CAN GET UP to 25 miles wide. It's the widest river in the world, but God's love is wider. The Great Wall of China is 13,170 miles long. It's so big it can be seen from outer space. But God's love is longer. Mount Everest is the highest mountain on earth, reaching over 29,000 feet high. But God's love is higher. The Grand Canyon is more than 6,000 feet deep, but God's love is deeper.

We use measuring sticks, scales, and tape measures to measure things on earth, but there isn't a tool big enough to measure God's love. That means God's love can't be blown away by bad news, stomped on by a bully or trauma, erased by a disorder or compulsion, or washed away by your mistakes. God's love is so great that it towers over everything else. And God offers this amazing love to you each and every day.

What's the tallest building or mountain you've ever seen? Could you reach the top? What's the deepest pool or lake you've ever swum in? Were you able to touch the bottom? Thank God for His vast love, and that you'll never be able to reach the top or bottom of it.

43

Jesus answered, "I am the way and the truth and the life.
No one comes to the Father except through me."

JOHN 14:6

WHAT IF YOU CAN'T DO IT? WHAT IF SOMETHING BAD HAP-pens? What if things don't work out? What if people think you're weird? You might have days when anxious or negative thoughts like these fill your mind. But that's all they are—thoughts. You have the power to take hold of them and do something with them, something other than panic, that is. You get to hold them up to the truth.

You can ask yourself, "Is that really true? Is it completely true?" Because maybe you can do that thing. Maybe something good will happen. Maybe everything will work out. And you don't know people will think you're weird. When you hold up anxious thoughts to the truth, you might find they're not worth worrying about at all.

Jesus is the truth. He calls Himself the truth. And He wants you to live in His truth—the truth that He loves you, forgives you, and doesn't judge your performance. In fact, He's right by your side cheering you on.

Dear Jesus, thank You for being the truth. Please help me stop negative thoughts in their tracks by holding them up to You. Please help me see the truth better so I can live a healthier, happier life. Amen.

"See, I am doing a new thing! Now it springs up; do you not perceive it?"
ISAIAH 43:19

ARE YOU IN A RUT? HAVE YOU GOTTEN IN THE HABIT OF retreating to your room if you don't want to deal with something or someone? Of maybe picking up your phone and scrolling to avoid conversations or doing the things you need to get done?

Maybe you haven't been getting the rest you need, because you stay up late binge-watching or maybe you've been sleeping way too much. There's good news. Today is a new day. A fresh start.

God wants the absolute best life for you, and He is always doing new things. Each day the sun rises again. The birds sing again. The calendar reads a new day of the week with a new date. And each day (that means even this one) you have the opportunity to break a bad habit and get in a new groove. If there's something you should change in your life—today is your day! You can get unstuck starting right now. Ready? Set? Go!

Dear God, thank You for doing new things all the time. Please provide me with the desire to do the things that are good for me and that glorify You. Amen.

DAY 46

"Do not seek revenge or bear a grudge against anyone among your people, but love your neighbor as yourself. I am the LORD."

LEVITICUS 19:18

FRIENDS. THEY'RE AWESOME. THEY'RE CHALLENGING. THEY'RE fun. They're great, until they're the worst. Because your friends are human, just like you, they'll mess up sometimes. Which means sometimes you mess up too. And when you put two people together who both make mistakes, some days there will be misunderstandings or arguments. Sometimes you'll let each other down or get on each other's nerves or feelings will get hurt. There will also be tons of laughter and great memories too. Just not all the time.

So how can you be a good friend? By treating others how you want to be treated. When one of your friends is driving you crazy, treat them how you would want to be treated if you were driving them crazy.

Would you want them to talk to you? Find a way to work through the problem? Forgive you for not being aware? Probably. If you like people to wait for you, listen to you, stand up for you, then do the same for your friends and for everyone you meet. Having good friends starts with being a good friend.

Is there someone you're struggling with? Think of three things you can do to treat them as you'd like to be treated. Tell them they did a good job or hold a door open for them. Find ways to do those three things this week.

*But the LORD said to Samuel, "Do not consider his appearance
or his height, for I have rejected him. The LORD does not
look at the things people look at. People look at the outward
appearance, but the LORD looks at the heart."*

1 SAMUEL 16:7

LOTS OF PEOPLE WILL TELL YOU WHO YOU ARE. THEY'LL assign labels and judge you based on your appearance or what kind of car you ride in. They'll tell you you're not fast enough, not strong enough, not smart enough, too loud, too quiet, too tall, or too short. But people aren't qualified to make those judgments. Only God has the right to tell you who or what you are. And God says you're priceless. God knows because He's who created you in the first place.

You could tell an elephant they were a starfish, but you wouldn't have the authority to do that, and you'd be totally wrong. Same with anyone who tries to tell you that you don't measure up, that you're not enough. Samuel was looking for a king. He found a man that he thought "looked" like a king. But God told Samuel how people look on the outside isn't what matters—it's what's inside. Jesus loves you and chooses you time and time again no matter what others say or think about you.

Look in the mirror and pick out your favorite feature. Thank God for your hair, smile, nose, freckles, whatever it is. Look again and realize that God's favorite feature is your heart. Thank God for always thinking you're amazing and worthy, just the way you are.

*And pray in the Spirit on all occasions with
all kinds of prayers and requests.*

EPHESIANS 6:18

GOD CALLS YOU HIS CHILD, HIS FRIEND, HIS BELOVED.
Those are all words we use to describe a relationship we have with
someone. And when we're in a relationship, we talk to the other
person. Kids and parents talk to each other. Friends chat with each
other. People who love each other communicate. You talk to someone to let them know how you're feeling, what you expect, what's
going on in your life, to share a story, to ask for help, or to get
encouragement.

If you believe that Jesus is your Savior, then you're in a relationship with God. He wants you to talk to Him. That's all prayer is.
You can talk to God anytime, anywhere, about everything. God
wants you to talk to Him about the test you're stressed about and
your current mood and the new kid in your group. God wants you
to thank Him, ask His opinion, and share with Him how you feel.
There isn't anything you can't talk to God about. The Bible says you
can talk to Him (pray) on all occasions with all kinds of prayers
and requests. Why not start now?

*Dear Jesus, thank You for wanting to talk to me, for wanting to
hear from me about everything, for being a safe place I can go
with all my problems and emotions. Here's what's on my mind
today: _____.*

Wonderful Counselor, Mighty God, Eternal Father, Prince of Peace.
ISAIAH 9:6 NASB

FEELING OVERWHELMED? THERE'S GOOD NEWS. WHEN you take a minute to look at the names of Jesus, of who He is and what He's capable of, you can start sorting all the crazy pieces of your life into a more organized, peaceful, and manageable place.

First, Jesus is a wonderful counselor. Anything you need to talk about? Jesus is an amazing listener who will give you the very best advice.

Next, He is mighty! Anything that needs to get done, Jesus can take care of it, because He has the authority to make the rules, change the rules, and the power and might to make sure that things get taken care of. There's no problem or issue too big for our mighty God.

Third, Jesus is our eternal Father. Imagine the very best dad—one who's strong, caring, available, understands you, and opens His arms wide to protect and comfort you.

Finally, He's the Prince of Peace. So when things feel anything but peaceful, Jesus can step in and calm things down, slow down the pace, and help you resume normal breathing.

Dear Jesus, thank You for Your wonderful, mighty, eternal, peaceful, loving self. Thank You for loving and protecting me. Help me hold on to the truth of who You are and what You're capable of. Amen.

Jesus said to him, "Receive your sight; your faith has healed you."
Immediately he received his sight and followed Jesus, praising God.

LUKE 18:42-43

IF SOMEONE THROWS YOU A BALL, YOU HAVE TO PUT your hands out to catch it or it will fall to the ground. If someone passes you the salt, you have to reach out and grab it or it will spill, and your food won't get seasoned.

Jesus offers you love, grace, forgiveness, strength, hope, peace, and encouragement. But you have to receive them. It's one thing to read these pages and say, "Oh great, Jesus loves me," or "Oh cool, God made me on purpose." It's another thing to truly receive these truths. To believe them. To put them into practice.

The next time you're feeling lonely, receive the truth that Jesus promises to be with you always (Matthew 28:20). The next time you have no idea what to do, receive the truth that God has great plans for you (Jeremiah 29:11). When you feel like you don't measure up, receive the truth that God created you wonderfully (Psalm 139:14). Are you ready to start truly receiving all the goodness God offers? Turn your hands over and open them up so they're facing the sky. Then pray the words below.

Dear Jesus, thank You for offering me love, grace, forgiveness, strength, hope, peace, and encouragement. Please help me 100 percent believe these truths. Help me receive all the gifts You offer and live in this goodness You give. Amen.

Praise him with timbrel and dancing.

PSALM 150:4

HOW COOL THAT THE BIBLE TELLS US TO DO THINGS THAT are fun, like dancing. Dancing is great for you. It's a kind of exercise, so everything that exercise does for you dance does for you, too, including improving the health of your heart. But dancing does so much more!

It increases your balance and strength. Dancing gives you a way to express yourself without words. It increases your ability to think. And dancing improves your mood.[4] Not to mention it can be a blast.

God wants you to enjoy yourself, express yourself, and take care of yourself. He invites you to dance as a way of praising Him. You could attend a fitness class like Zumba, watch the music video for your favorite upbeat song and try to do the steps with the dancers, go on a social media app that provides instructions and record your own, play a dancing video game, or simply crank up some tunes and dance around your family room. Grabbing a friend to join in the dance party is always a plus.

Dear God, thank You for creating music and dance. Thank You for wanting me to have fun and giving me ways to do that. Amen.

"I have told you these things, so that in me you may have peace. In this world you will have trouble. But take heart! I have overcome the world."

JOHN 16:33

DO YOU FEEL OVERWHELMED? STRESSED OUT? LIKE YOU could use a hug? We all do sometimes. You might lose a game, your homework, or your phone. You might run out of time with a long list of things you still need to do. People you care about might let you down or leave. Some days you ache inside or feel super jittery.

Jesus completely understands. He experienced all kinds of trouble while He was here on earth. God made you, loves you, and understands exactly what you're going through. Jesus offers you peace. He knows hard stuff will come your way, but He promises to help you overcome it. That could be with something as simple as a hug or something more complex like the right prescription or therapist.

You can have peace in Jesus, because all the awful, painful, challenging things of the world—Jesus has overcome them all. Step into His arms. Lean into Him. Breathe in His peace.

Draw a peace sign. In each of the four openings write something you're worried about or overwhelmed by. Turn each thing over to Jesus. Ask Him to take control of whatever's going on. Then draw a cross over each of the things and breathe in the peace and help Jesus is offering.

For all of you who were baptized into Christ
have clothed yourselves with Christ.
GALATIANS 3:27

EACH MORNING YOU GET TO DECIDE WHAT YOU PUT ON. Depending on what the weather is like and where you're going, it changes from day to day. Today might be a sweatpants or joggers kind of day. Or maybe you need to wear your uniform for a game or get dressed up for a special occasion. But something you should put on every morning is Jesus.

How do you wear Jesus? Well, think about your clothes—they protect you, they're the closest things next to you, and they're what everybody else sees when they look at you. So, when you start your day with Jesus,—"Clothe yourself in Him"—ask Him to protect you today from shame, worries, and fears. Tell Jesus you want Him to be the closest thing next to you today.

No matter where you go or who you see today, try to do and say what Jesus would so everyone around you sees His love when they look at you. Get the idea? Jesus is better than any outfit you own, because when you clothe yourself in Christ, you are complete.

As you're getting dressed today, talk to Jesus. Ask Him to protect, cover, stay close to, and shine through you throughout your day. Then whatever comes your way today, keep reminding yourself you are clothed in Christ.

DAY 54

> *"Suppose one of you has a hundred sheep and loses one*
> *of them. Doesn't he leave the ninety-nine in the open*
> *country and go after the lost sheep until he finds it?"*
>
> LUKE 15:4–5

HAVE YOU EVER LOST SOMETHING IMPORTANT AND scrambled around to find it? Some days you might feel like you're losing everything! Do you get a little stressed when you can't find it? Digging through drawers, searching under your bed? Asking everyone you know if they've seen it?

How do you feel when you find it? Relieved? Happy? Grateful? You probably only act that way if the missing item was really important. Right? You certainly wouldn't put that much effort into finding a wrapper.

Think how hard you search for something important when it's missing. That's how intently Jesus seeks you. He wants to support you every single day. Anytime you ignore Him or wander off from Him, Jesus starts His search for you all over again, and He won't stop until He finds you. You're that important to Him. No matter how far away you've gone or how lost you've become, Jesus will drop everything to find you. And when He finds you, He'll celebrate.

Sit in a quiet place, close your eyes, and ask God to find you. Ask Him to sit and talk with you. Tell Him you're sorry for any time you've wandered off, and thank Him for always coming to look for you. Ask Him to help you stay close to Him all the time.

*Finally, brothers and sisters, whatever is true, whatever
is noble, whatever is right, whatever is pure, whatever is
lovely, whatever is admirable—if anything is excellent
or praiseworthy—think about such things.*
PHILIPPIANS 4:8

CAN WE TALK ABOUT WHAT YOU'VE BEEN WATCHING, LIS-
tening to, and posting? Is it right? Is it pure? Is it lovely? Is it true?

The more you expose yourself to ugly words, suggestive pictures, or people making bad choices, the more those things will
seem normal to you. Maybe it seems like everyone you know
watches "that show" or listens to "that artist," but that doesn't
make it okay. If a movie makes you uncomfortable, don't watch
it. If a song has bad lyrics, stop listening. If you know in your gut
that picture or text isn't right or admirable—don't post or send it.

God wants the best for you. He'll help you achieve all kinds
of great things, but God wants you to do your part. When you fill
your ears, eyes, heart, and mind with excellent, admirable, praiseworthy things, you'll be able to experience God's love more fully,
because there will be less of that other noise drowning Him out.

Today, find a way to cut one bad influence out of your life. Maybe it
means deleting a song or unfollowing someone. Maybe it means
you need to tell a friend who has been pressuring you to do bad
things that you need space. Ask God for the courage to pursue
what is right.

> *"Be strong and courageous. Do not be afraid or terrified*
> *because of them, for the LORD your God goes with*
> *you; he will never leave you nor forsake you."*
>
> DEUTERONOMY 31:6

PETER PARKER WAS AN ORDINARY TEENAGER. ONE DAY HE got bit by a radioactive spider and gained superpowers. He became strong, lightning fast, and his senses were heightened. With his new powers he became courageous and took down all kinds of bad guys. His new powers allowed him to do the impossible.

Just like Spider-Man, you can do the impossible. Not because you have superpowers, but because you have something way better—God.

Think you can't make it through this year in science? You can. Because with God you are strong. Not sure how you could possibly adjust to the major changes going on in your life? You can. God is more powerful than anything or anyone and He will never, ever leave you. With God at your side you can tackle anything and everything that comes your way.

You are strong. You are courageous. That's how God made you.

What are you afraid of today? Imagine that thing or person is just a thin, stringy spiderweb. Now imagine yourself carrying that web and laying it down at God's feet. Ask God to take this fear from you. Ask Him to help you to live in the strength and courage He gives you.

The steward agreed to [let Daniel and his friends eat a healthy diet] and fed them vegetables and water for ten days. At the end of the ten days they looked better and more robust than all the others who had been eating from the royal menu.

DANIEL 1:14-16 MSG

THANKFULLY YOU DON'T HAVE TO EAT ONLY VEGETABLES and drink only water, but Daniel, the guy famous for surviving the lions' den, was onto something. We're not sure why he didn't want to eat from the royal menu, but something about it felt wrong to him. And so Daniel simply asked the person in charge of meals if he could eat something else.

You have this power too. To avoid things that are unhealthy for you. This could be saying "no" to cheese if you're lactose intolerant, "no" to alcohol when peers are drinking, or "no" to the super-sized fries. Scientists have proven that eating healthy is good not only for your body but also for your mind. More importantly, God created your body and your mind. Use your power of "no" today to eat right, practice healthy living, and be mindful of your mental health.

Dear God, thank You for creating my mind and body. Please give me the courage to say "no" when necessary and help me make healthy choices and enable me to do all the wonderful things You have planned for me. Amen.

When Jesus reached the spot, he looked up and said to him, "Zacchaeus, come down immediately. I must stay at your house today."

LUKE 19:5

YOU PROBABLY HAVE A LOT GOING ON IN YOUR LIFE. YOU have family, friends, and school. You might be involved in activities, youth group, sports, or band. You are most likely responsible for things around your house, or volunteer work. Some days you're probably great at some or all those things. Some days you might mess up. When you're doing all those things, do you ever wonder if Jesus really sees you? If He really knows what's going on with you? If He cares?

He does.

The gospel writer Luke tells us about a not very nice man named Zacchaeus who climbed a tree so he could get a good view of Jesus and no one would see him. Or so he thought. But Jesus saw Zacchaeus in those branches. Jesus stopped, looked up, and called out to Zacchaeus. Jesus told Zacchaeus He was coming over to his house to hang out with him.

Jesus does this for you too. Wherever you are. Whatever you're doing—good or bad, busy or bored. Jesus notices you. He cares about you and wants to hang out with you.

Dear Jesus, thank You for seeing, noticing, and caring about me. Thank You for wanting to hang out with me. Help me be more aware of Your presence and love. Amen.

"I have come that they may have life, and have it to the full."
JOHN 10:10

WOULD YOU RATHER HAVE JUST ONE BITE OF YOUR favorite pizza or a whole slice? Would you rather get to watch ten minutes of the newest episode of your favorite show or all of it? Would you rather have to sleep in a corner of your bed every night or have the full bed?

Jesus came so that you could have a full life. Not a partial life or a so-so life. This doesn't mean you always get the whole couch or the entire pan of lasagna to yourself, but it does mean that God wants you to have a full life—full of peace, full of joy, full of love.

You don't have to earn it. You don't have to prove yourself. You don't have to pay for it. It's all there waiting for you right now. All you have to do is tell Jesus you love Him, and you want the full life He offers.

Then you can prepare to be overwhelmed with the amazing, full life He has waiting for you.

Dear Jesus, thank You for offering me such a full life, that I don't have to do anything except ask You for it. I'm asking You now—I love You. I want this life overflowing with peace, joy, and love. Amen.

Whoever is kind to the poor lends to the LORD, and
he will reward them for what they have done.

PROVERBS 19:17

SCIENTISTS HAVE DISCOVERED THAT IF YOU HELP PEOPLE
on a regular basis, you'll be calmer, have better health, less depression, and might even live longer![5] This makes sense. God created
everyone, and He wants all His people to be loved and cared for—
that includes you. This verse from Proverbs says you'll be rewarded
for helping those in need. And it's true!

God invites you into His beautiful plan of caring for others,
so help someone else today. Help your dad unload the groceries. Donate your allowance to a local fundraiser. Do one of your
sibling's chores or help them with their homework. Or maybe volunteer at a local charity or at your church. If you don't know where
to start, ask a parent, teacher, or pastor for ideas. When you take
time to give to or care for others, an amazing thing happens—a
"feel good" chemical is released in your brain. God uses your kindness to help others and you.

Dear God, thank You for creating everyone in the world. There
are so many people in need. Please show me ways I can help
others and share Your love and light with them. Amen.

"If you have faith as small as a mustard seed, you can say to this mulberry tree, 'Be uprooted and planted in the sea,' and it will obey you."

LUKE 17:6

IS IT HARD TO BELIEVE IN THINGS YOU CAN'T SEE? IT doesn't have to be. You can't see love, but you probably know someone who loves you. You know how their love feels—how it can change you. You believe love is real and that it has power.

You can't see the wind, but you can feel its presence. You can see how it scatters leaves, bends trees, and waves flags. You believe wind is real and that it has power.

You may not be able to see God, but you don't need to see Him to know what He feels like, to see how He can make a difference in your life. Still, some days—days when you're riddled with anxiety, get bad news, are flooded with depression, or when someone breaks your confidence—it may be difficult to have faith. Luckily, God doesn't ask you to have much faith—just the teeniest, tiniest bit, smaller than a kernel of popcorn. And if you have just a tiny speck of faith, then with God you can do anything.

Go outside. Notice the weather. Soak in the warmth or the chill, feel the sunlight, wind, or drops of rain on your skin. Marvel at how you cannot see warm, cold, wind, or wet, yet all of them are real. Thank God for His very real presence in your life.

DAY 62

Shout for joy to the LORD, all the earth, burst
into jubilant song with music.

PSALM 98:4

WHAT MAKES YOU LAUGH OUT LOUD? WHO MAKES YOU smile? If you had an extra thirty minutes today, what would you do to make yourself happy? God created things He knew would personally delight you. Are you doing any of those things today? If not, what's stopping you?

Yes, some days are hard, harsh, and even depressing. When things are serious, you shouldn't blow them off or pretend they didn't happen. But you do have the power to flip your mood from bored to engaged, from so-so to joyful, from grumpy to glad. How? By doing something that sounds fun to you—that makes you "shout for joy."

God wants you to do things that make you happy and spend time with people you love. God loves you so much. He wants you to dance, sing, and cheer!

You don't need permission to have fun—you just need to get out there and do it.

Go for a bike ride and let the wind blow through your hair. Or maybe message someone who makes you smile and set up a time to hang out. If sporting events get you pumped, go cheer on a local team. While you're at it, make sure to thank God for bikes, friends, sports, or whatever brings you joy.

In the beginning God created the heavens and the earth.

GENESIS 1:1

A RECENT POLL DETERMINED THE AVERAGE AMERICAN will spend forty-four years of their lives in front of an electronic screen![6] Geesh! There's nothing wrong with watching a great movie, doing homework on a device, checking social media, or texting someone on your phone, but forty-four years?

In the beginning God created the heavens and the earth. And they're still there. But most of the world is spending way more time on their screens than outside. Too much screen time can lead to headaches, blurred vision, and struggles falling asleep. Who wants that?

So get outside today—away from the screens and back to the beautiful creation God made. Be creative. Toss a ball with your brother, take your sketch pad outdoors, or suggest your family have a picnic in your yard or at a park. If it's hot, you could go swimming at a pool or wading in a creek. If it's freezing, you could bundle up and go for a hike, make a snowman, or go sledding. Do something—anything—outside.

Dear Jesus, thank You for creating the world! There is so much out there to see and experience. Please help me find ways to take breaks from screens and explore the beautiful nature You made. Amen.

DAY 64

LONG AGO IT WAS DANGEROUS FOR SHIPS TO BE OUT AT sea. If they were lost, they couldn't call for directions. If they were sinking, they couldn't contact help. When the telegraph was invented, it provided ships with a way to call for rescue, no matter how far from land they were.

Dot-dot-dot. Dash-dash-dash. Dot-dot-dot.

That combination of dots and dashes translate into the letters "S-O-S" in Morse code (the alphabet of the telegraph). In 1908, SOS was chosen as the international distress signal,[7] similar to our 911.

If you feel like you're sinking, you don't need a telegraph. You don't need to know Morse code. You have God. And He hears you. Contacting Him is way easier than typing SOS. All you have to do is say His name. God hears you no matter how far lost you feel, no matter how far from Him you've sailed, even if you feel like you're drowning. God hears you and He'll rescue you.

Dots in Morse code are quick taps. Dashes are long taps. Think of something you want to talk to God about. Try praying while tapping out an SOS to Him. Dot-dot-dot. Dash-dash-dash. Dot-dot-dot. It's like a drumbeat. With each tap, know that God will always hear your cry.

"Who shows no partiality to princes and does not favor the rich over the poor, for they are all the work of his hands?"

JOB 34:19

DOES IT SEEM LIKE THE KIDS WHOSE FAMILIES KNOW THE volleyball coach get the most playing time? Like the kids who live in that neighborhood have the coolest gym shoes, backpacks, or cars? Does it feel like everyone wants to be a part of that group of friends?

In your day-to-day life, some people might get preferential treatment over others. But God doesn't work like that. God doesn't judge you by what you wear, where you live, or who your friends are. God doesn't rate you by your grades, your haircut, or what activities you are or aren't involved in. God made you with His own hands. He made you exactly how you are, and He loves you exactly how you are. He picks you for His lineup and to play in His band. If God had a screen saver, your face would be in the picture. It's hard to imagine that God loves all His children. But it's true. That includes you. God loves you!

Make a list of your favorite things—favorite color, flavor of ice cream, maybe your favorite team, song, or book. Think of how fantastic all the things on your list make you feel. Know that God feels the same way when He thinks about you. Thank God for loving you that much.

DAY 66

Teach us to number our days, that we may gain a heart of wisdom.

PSALM 90:12

DO YOU EVER COUNT DOWN THE DAYS UNTIL CHRISTMAS, your birthday, or a day off school? Does it sometimes seem to take for-e-ver, like the days are passing by in slow motion?

Every day God wants to teach you something, share something with you, and have you experience something wonderful. The days leading up to Christmas are full of decorating, baking (and eating) cookies, or belting out Christmas songs. It's all part of the fun. You wouldn't want to skip those things, would you? God is excited for our celebrations, but with God every single day counts. God will use every practice to prepare you for games and every rehearsal to help you learn your lines for opening night. In the same way God will use every single day of your life to allow you to discover delicious flavors, have interesting conversations, meet new people, discover amazing things, be comforted by hugs, and experience quiet moments in which He can remind you how much He loves you.

No matter what you're looking forward to, make sure you're not overlooking where you are today and what God might be doing in it.

Dear Jesus, thank You for today. Please show me ways to enjoy today, tomorrow, and every day—even the ones I'm counting down to something else. Amen.

But you are a chosen people, a royal priesthood, a holy nation,
God's special possession, that you may declare the praises of him
who called you out of darkness into his wonderful light.

1 PETER 2:9

IN A PRESIDENTIAL ELECTION THE COUNTRY GETS TO vote for who they want as president—for who they think the best person is to lead their country. At school, you might get to vote for student council members. You're supposed to vote for who you think will best represent your class. A club might get to vote for a leader, someone the club members believe will guide the club with a great attitude and work ethic. The people elected, those who win the vote, are chosen.

So are you. But you are chosen by someone far more important than your classmates, members of your club, or even than the population of your country. You are chosen by God. God votes for you. God picks you. Every single day, He fills out His ballot and says, "You, you're the one I want to love. You're the one I think is special. You're the one I want to help. You're the one I want to spend time with today."

You are chosen by God. Let that sink in.

Look in the mirror and say out loud, "I am chosen by God. I am royal and holy in God's eyes. I am God's special possession." Write at least one of those phrases on a sticky note and put it on your mirror to remind you again how awesome God thinks you are.

I was pushed back and about to fall, but the LORD helped me. The LORD is my strength and my defense; he has become my salvation.

PSALM 118:13-14

HAVE YOU EVER TRIPPED AND FELT SUPER EMBARRASSED? Ever had a stain on your shirt and had to walk around all day with a big spot, feeling self-conscious? Have you ever not had enough money to go to the game or see the movie and not wanted anyone to know? Have you ever responded with the wrong answer when the teacher called on you?

Embarrassing moments happen. But if you remember that Jesus has your back, you can let these uncomfortable moments go. You don't have to hold on to them. Jesus isn't judging your clothes, sense of balance, what you can afford, or if you "fit in." He loves you, always.

Impressing others isn't the most important thing. Jesus is. He already thinks you're awesome. When you let this truth really sink in, you can shake off a mistake, get back up with the LORD's strength, apologize if you've bumped someone, and maybe even laugh at the awkward moments fully confident that God will love you no matter what.

Imagine Jesus next to you during an embarrassing moment. If you dropped your food in the cafeteria, picture Jesus helping clean up your mess. Thank Jesus for having your back. For being your strength and salvation.

Each one should test their own actions. Then they can take pride in themselves alone, without comparing themselves to someone else.

GALATIANS 6:4

SOCIAL MEDIA CAN BE GREAT—INSPIRING PICTURES AND quotes, catching up with people you love and ideas that matter. Seeing what your favorite influencers are up to. But it can also be dangerous. If you start rating yourself or your life based on what others are doing, you'll lose sight of the incredible person God created you to be.

Most people post highlights—the time they won the award, nailed their workout, or visited an awesome place. Few post about failing a test, taking out the trash, missing someone, or feeling vulnerable. What you see on social media is only what others want you to see. The kids who went to the concert could be experiencing personal problems. The pictures they posted would never let you in on those things.

No matter what others post, no matter how many hearts or likes you do or don't get on your social media, you are loved and cherished by the Creator of the universe. Comparisons are pointless, because you've already been liked, hearted, and retweeted by the King of kings.

If you're on social media, post something about Jesus today—your favorite Bible verse, or something awesome He created. Thank Jesus for that wonderful thing or person in your post. If you're not on social media, tell someone, "I'm thankful that Jesus . . ."

> *Not giving up meeting together, as some are in the*
> *habit of doing, but encouraging one another.*

HEBREWS 10:25

WHEN YOU HAVE A BAD DAY, DO POORLY ON A TEST, GET in an argument with a friend, how do you react? Do you run off by yourself? Shut your door? Isolate yourself when you're still in a group by focusing on your phone instead of the people around you?

Everybody needs a moment (or ten) alone. But it can be dangerous to isolate ourselves. When you close yourself off from others, the dark days feel darker and the struggles more intense.

God created us to be with other people. You shouldn't share with everyone, every time, but when you engage in a safe space with people you trust, those people can cheer you on, remind you that you're not alone, help you sort out the hard stuff, show you how awesome you truly are, and point you back to God's goodness and truth, of how much He loves you.

Share a struggle with a trusted Christian friend or family member. Not sure who? Try attending a youth group or Bible study or seek out someone who you know loves God. Start with something small and let God use someone else to encourage you.

*"I am the Alpha and the Omega," says the LORD God, "who
is, and who was, and who is to come, the Almighty."*

REVELATION 1:8

IN MOST MOVIES AND BOOKS, THE BEGINNINGS AND ends are the most important parts—they're the parts that show you what the story is going to be about and how all the pieces finally fit together.

When you were little, you probably learned the alphabet song. Even when you weren't sure what order all the letters went in, you probably got A and Z right—the beginning and the end. In the Greek alphabet, alpha is like our letter "A" and omega is like our "Z."

God said, "I am the A and the Z—the beginning and the end. I'm why and how it all got started—the world, your life, everything. I'm also how all the pieces fit together, how the problems get solved, how the wrongs are made right, how everything makes sense." God was with the world before it was created, is with you every second right now, and will be with all of creation to the very end. Find strength and comfort in His security and constant presence today.

In the notes section, write out your ABCs, but replace "A" and "Z" with the word "God." Now write three sentences about yourself and replace any "a" or "z" with God's name. Notice how important He is to your life and thank Him for being the God who's always there.

DAY 72

SIMONE BILES, ONE OF THE MOST SUCCESSFUL GYM-
nasts of all time, shocked the world when she withdrew from the
2020 Olympics stating, "I have to focus on my mental health and
not jeopardize my health and well-being."[8] Biles had been predicted
to win the gold. Can you imagine the pressure between competing
and stepping down to take care of yourself? At the Olympics? How
could she possibly make such a decision? Simone has something
she uses as a compass to guide her. Earlier she said, "I was taught
that you can go to Him [God] for anything and He's the one that
directs your life."

You can do the same. You can go to God when you don't know
what to do, when you're worried about your physical or mental
health, when it feels like people are counting on you, when you've
worked so hard. God is listening. He cares so much about you. You
can go to God with all your requests.

*Dear God, please help me with all the decisions I need to make,
specifically about _____. Please keep me from being
anxious about the possible outcomes. Please flood me with Your
peace and show me what to do. Amen.*

*Every good and perfect gift is from above, coming down from the Father
of the heavenly lights, who does not change like shifting shadows.*

JAMES 1:17

DO YOU HAVE A PULSE TODAY? DID YOU EAT ANYTHING?
Are you wearing clothes? Of course, those are things you expect
each day, that are part of your day, but can you imagine your life
without air, food, or clothing? Every single gift you experience
comes from God—everything.

It's God's gift when the sun shines through a window provid-
ing you light. When an adorable squirrel skitters across your path,
or your teacher brings doughnuts to class. When there's still hot
water when it's your turn to take a shower. When you understand
the new concept in math. When your pillow feels soft under your
head. These are all gifts from God.

And yes, bad things happen. But God will sprinkle good and
perfect gifts into your day to remind you that He cares, He's on
your side, and He's always with you. Keep your eye out for the gifts
God gives you today.

Did you start a gratitude journal on Day 39? If so, pull it out now
or maybe start one now. Throughout the day jot down the gifts you
notice God has given you. Make a habit of it. Challenge yourself to
add to it every day this week.

Honesty guides good people;
dishonesty destroys treacherous people.

PROVERBS 11:3 NLT

IF YOU ACCIDENTALLY BROKE A GLASS IN THE KITCHEN, would you tell your parents? If you forgot to do an assignment, would you tell your teacher or would you make up an excuse? If a friend wanted you to come over and you were super tired, would you tell them you were exhausted, or say you weren't allowed to go out?

It's not always easy to tell the truth—especially if you don't want to hurt someone's feelings, get in trouble, or be embarrassed. But telling the truth is what God wants you to do. Honestly, it's what you want other people to do for you. Jesus says He is the way, the truth, and the life (John 14:6). He is actual truth, and He wants to help guide you to tell the truth too. Because when you tell the truth, you can live in freedom of that truth, never having to stress out about being found out. Don't worry, Jesus loves you even though you've probably bent the truth or lied before (everyone has). Jesus loves you no matter what. And because He loves you so much, He wants what's best for you, including the freedom of an honest life.

Dear Jesus, please forgive me for all the times I've lied in the past.
Please give me the courage to tell the truth in all circumstances.
Thank You for being truth I can always count on. Amen.

So we fix our eyes not on what is seen, but on what is unseen,
since what is seen is temporary, but what is unseen is eternal.
2 CORINTHIANS 4:18

THE PEOPLE OF ANCIENT POMPEII HAD A HEATED POOL, crosswalks, and fast-food restaurants. Pretty amazing considering they lived almost two thousand years ago! They thought they had everything, but in the end none of their stuff could save them. In AD 79, the entire population of Pompeii died instantly when Mount Vesuvius erupted.

Today there are volcanologists who can predict when volcanoes will erupt—which saves so many lives. But modern culture is still hooked on having the latest and greatest of everything. There's absolutely nothing wrong with getting new and improved things—with enjoying what life has to offer—but when things become more important than God, there's a problem.

Even though you may see the coolest new clothes in a store, or the latest phone in your friend's pocket, there's nothing cooler than Jesus. Everything else becomes outdated, or eventually needs to be replaced. Stay focused on Jesus. He'll be with you through any unexpected storm, will hold you when things spin out of control, and will never need an update.

What are your most valued possessions? Go through your list one by one and tell Jesus you want to love Him more—more than possessions. Thank Jesus for always being there for you and for lasting forever.

You live under the freedom of God's grace.
ROMANS 6:14 NLT

DO YOU EVER PUT PRESSURE ON YOURSELF? TO GET IT all right? To have all the answers in class, run the drill correctly in practice, play the game just right, hit the right note, wear the right outfit, post the perfect post on social media, or say the right thing? Do you ever stress about if you're doing what God wants you to do?

Those are all great goals. God wants you to do your best—to use the tools and talents He's given you to glorify Him. If God made you a musician, He loves it when you hit the right note. If God gave you an understanding of technology, He thinks it's awesome when you code something new. God wants you to be kind, tell the truth, share, and avoid things that are bad for your physical or mental health. But God also offers you so much grace—endless grace. God doesn't expect you to do things perfectly. He knows you'll mess up. That doesn't anger or disappoint Him. He extends you the freedom of grace to try again, or let it go, or start over. He loves you no matter what.

Dear Jesus, thank You for Your amazing grace. Let me exhale the pressures of this world and breathe in Your grace today. Help me live in the freedom Your grace gives. Amen.

David said to the Philistine, "You come against me with sword and spear and javelin, but I come against you in the name of the LORD Almighty, the God of the armies of Israel, whom you have defied."

1 SAMUEL 17:45

FOUGHT ANY BATTLES LATELY? AND NO, VIDEO GAMES don't count. Everyone fights battles sometimes. Battles against poverty, racism, a mental or physical disorder, being misunderstood, fatigue, hurt feelings, or not being given a chance. But here's the good news. You don't have to be afraid because you don't have to fight your battles alone. Not a single one of them.

There was once a young guy named David. He was a shepherd. Not a warrior. He went against the biggest champion the enemy had in their army. That guy was an actual giant with an assistant and major weapons. David only had five rocks and a slingshot. But David wasn't afraid. Why? Because he knew God was on his side. He fully believed it. David took that giant down with his slingshot.

God is on your side too. You don't have to own the latest technology, have tons of money, or know the right people, because you have God. And with Him by your side you can stand strong against any battle you face.

Dear God, thank You for being on my side. Thank You for being mightier than anything or anyone I face. Please help me turn my emotions and fears over to You as I invite You to fight my battles for me today. Amen.

77

Remember the Sabbath day by keeping it holy.
EXODUS 20:8

SCIENCE SHOWS US THAT A DAY OFF EACH WEEK REDUCES stress, helps you focus, adds years to your life, increases your creativity, and helps your immune system fight off germs and viruses.[9] But long before scientists researched the benefits of taking a day off, God created the original day off—Sabbath—and asked us to practice it.

Do you take any days off? From your schoolwork? Your training? Your lessons? Do you take a day off every week to relax and unwind? When you keep going and going a million miles an hour, you can get run-down and stressed out. You no longer function at full strength.

God created Sabbath. Not for Himself. He's God. He doesn't get tired or worn out or need a break. He created it for humans, because people need to rest, recharge, and refuel. God designed your body to run, play, think, work, and problem solve, but also to rest so you can do all those other things even better.

Schedule a day off this week. If you can't take an entire day, try a morning or afternoon to truly rest. Rest could include things like sleeping, going on a walk, reading a book, grabbing tacos with a friend, or drawing. Find something that helps you unwind in a healthy way and commit to it.

The angel said to those who were standing before him, "Take off his filthy clothes." Then he said to Joshua, "See, I have taken away your sin, and I will put fine garments on you."
ZECHARIAH 3:4

HAVE YOU EVER GOTTEN HOT AND SWEATY OR FILTHY? How soon did you shower and change? If you didn't have time to clean up right away, how did you feel? Sticky? Itchy? Gross?

That's the same way it feels if you stay in your sin. But you don't have to. If you feel bad about something, ask Jesus for forgiveness. He instantly and completely forgives you.

Feeling guilty about making a bad choice, hurting someone's feelings, or sneaking something you know is bad for you is natural. It's a reminder that God is good, and He longs for you to be like Him. It should motivate you to do better next time. But those shameful feelings should last only until you tell Jesus you're sorry. Then you can let them go. Jesus does. He wants you to learn from your mistakes, not dwell on them. Ask Him for forgiveness and accept His amazing grace.

1. Imagine yourself wearing dirty clothes. Label the clothes with anything you're struggling forgiving yourself for (or maybe a mistake you repeatedly seem to make).
2. Imagine Jesus handing you clean clothes.
3. Imagine yourself throwing your grubby clothes in the trash, never to be seen again, and putting on the fresh outfit Christ offers.

*"My sheep listen to my voice; I know them, and they
follow me. I give them eternal life, and they shall never
perish; no one will snatch them out of my hand."*

JOHN 10:27-28

SHEEP REACT TO THEIR SHEPHERD'S VOICE. ANOTHER person can say the same words, the same phrases, in the same language as their shepherd, and the sheep won't respond. Why? Because sheep know their shepherd personally. They trust him. They know he will lead them to fresh grass to eat. Sheep know their shepherd will chase off wolves and keep them safe.

Jesus called Himself the Good Shepherd because He has your best interests in mind. He'll keep you safe and guide you where you need to go. Listen for His voice so when He calls, you'll know which way to go. When He's warning you, you'll be able to avoid trouble.

The more time you spend with Jesus, the more you'll recognize His voice. The more you read the Bible, talk to Him, tell Him what's on your mind, what's stressing you out, what you're excited about, who it's hard to be nice to, what emotions you're feeling, the more you'll get familiar with Jesus' voice. Talk to Him today.

Chat with Jesus. Thank Him for something great or share something you're struggling with. Sit quietly and let Him respond. You might feel warm or safe or relieved. You might think of something to do or someone to hug.

Finally, be strong in the LORD and in his mighty power. Put on the full armor of God, so that you can take your stand against the devil's schemes.

EPHESIANS 6:10-11

SOME DAYS ARE REALLY HARD—WHEN YOU'RE SICK IN BED, feeling horrible, missing school, and worrying that you'll fall behind. When someone you love moves away or passes away and your heart really misses them. What do you do?

Jesus says, "Here, put on my armor. It will protect you."

What is the armor of God? It's described in Ephesians 6 as the belt of truth, breastplate of righteousness, shoes of peace, shield of faith, helmet of salvation, and sword of the Spirit.

You can stand in the truth that God loves you and is for you, that He already calls you holy and forgiven. You can breathe in Christ's peace. Hold up your shield of faith, believing all these things are true. Put on your helmet of salvation, remembering Jesus has saved you and will continue to save you, and wave around the sword, the words from the Bible, to remind yourself of God's faithfulness. Jesus gives you all these things—His own armor—so you can stand up to anything that comes your way.

Dear Jesus, thank You for Your armor. Please help me remember that it's all there for me to use anytime, anywhere. Thank You for Your truth, righteousness, peace, faith, and salvation, and for the Bible. I am so grateful. Amen.

Each of you should use whatever gift you have received to serve others, as faithful stewards of God's grace in its various forms.

1 PETER 4:10

WHAT ARE YOU GOOD AT? DO YOU KNOW GOD IS THE reason you're good at that thing?

Are you a musician? You might practice your instrument for hours on end, but God gave you that love of music, put you in a home or school where someone encouraged you to play, gave you access to lessons and to an instrument. So play for Him.

What does that mean? It means not groaning when you must practice, but instead considering it a privilege that God gave you this gift. Maybe play "Happy Birthday" for your grandpa's birthday, volunteer to play at a nursing home, or help a younger sibling learn how to read music.

Are you awesome at tennis? God gave you a love for playing and resources to be able to take lessons and access courts. He also gave you strength and physical ability. Play for Him. Teach a younger player how to swing a racket. Play fairly. Show God's love to the people you play with and against.

You get the idea—whatever you're great at, God made you that way. Do it for Him!

Dear Jesus, thank You so much for making me good at _____. Please help me use this gift to glorify You and make Your world a better place. Amen.

"This, then, is how you should pray: 'Our Father in heaven, hallowed be your name, your kingdom come, your will be done, on earth as it is in heaven.'"

MATTHEW 6:9-10

NO MATTER WHAT'S GOING ON TODAY, YOU CAN TALK TO God. You don't need any tools or to have any Bible verses memorized. You don't need to be at church or know certain words. You can talk to God right where you are out loud or in your head about anything and everything.

Not sure where to start? Jesus explains what prayer can look like in Matthew 6:9–13. This is often called the "LORD's Prayer" or the "Our Father." You can say it word for word if you want, use it as an outline, or as a way to get started with prayer. Tell God you think He's great. Tell Him you want things to go His way, because you believe His ways are best. Ask God for whatever you need—anything. You can be vulnerable with Him. He's safe. Ask for forgiveness for anything you feel bad about. Ask God to help you forgive anyone you're upset with. And ask God to protect you from doing bad things and from bad things coming your way. Pretty simple, really. The important thing is that God wants to hear from you.

Dear God, thank You for wanting to talk with me. Here are some things I'm thankful for: _____. Here are some things I could use help with: _____. You are so good. I love You. Amen.

*Many waters cannot quench love; rivers cannot sweep
it away. If one were to give all the wealth of one's
house for love, it would be utterly scorned.*

SONG OF SOLOMON 8:7

GOD'S LOVE FOR YOU IS HUGE. EVEN IF YOU WANTED TO, you couldn't outrun God's love. You couldn't jump higher than it or outthink it. A tornado couldn't blow God's love away from you. The strongest power lifter couldn't pull God's love away from you. The richest person in the world couldn't pay God to stop loving you.

This also means no evil rumor can take God's love from you. No nasty social media post can stop God from loving you. Nothing you've done or mistake you've made could make God stop loving you. No snide comment. No backstabbing frenemy or toxic family member could ever convince God to stop loving you. Nothing and no one could make Him stop loving you, because God created you.

Write yourself a loving note or song from God, reminding yourself how much He loves you. Put it somewhere you'll see it—the inside cover of your notebook, in your locker, or in your sock drawer. Each time you see it, thank God for loving you. Remember to tell Him you love Him too.

Peter and the other apostles replied: "We must obey God rather than human beings!"

ACTS 5:29

WHEN YOUR FRIENDS SEND EACH OTHER PICTURES OF their homework, that's cheating. When your teammates cut corners on the laps they're running, that's cheating. When your sister says, "Mom and Dad are out—they'll never know we watched this movie," that's sneaky. When you have a secret social media account or profile or you delete a text so your parents won't see it, that's also sneaky.

It doesn't matter if the problem is hard, your legs are tired, or the rule seems dumb to you. It doesn't matter if everyone else is doing it. Down in your gut you know right from wrong, and God calls you to be honest. Not to punish you. He knows that your life will be better if you learn, get stronger, stay safe, and avoid negative images and people.

Who are you trying to please? God? Or the world? When you follow Jesus and the way of life He patterned for you, your life will be more full of love, joy, hope, peace, and grace.

Dear Jesus, thank You for always knowing exactly what's going on in my life. Please forgive me when I choose to please other people instead of You. Thank You for always knowing what's best and wanting the best for me. Please give me strength and faith to follow You no matter what others do. Amen.

"Share your food with the hungry, and give shelter to
the homeless. Give clothes to those who need them, and
do not hide from relatives who need your help."

ISAIAH 58:7 NLT

IF YOU HAVE A ROOF OVER YOUR HEAD, A PLACE TO SLEEP, food in your fridge, and clothes on your back, you are richer than 75 percent of the world! It's hard to imagine that so many teens your age literally don't have a place to sleep or food to eat. But it's true.

That means:

1. You have a lot to thank God for, and . . .
2. You can help God's children who aren't as fortunate as you.

Volunteering is the perfect way to do both. Talk to a parent, teacher, or pastor to get suggestions on how you can make a difference. Some ideas are collecting for a food pantry, helping a team of adults deliver gifts at Christmas, volunteering with your youth group to pass out food or blankets to the homeless, or writing letters to people who need a friend. There are so many more! When you serve others in need, you are reminded of how fortunate you are, and you share God's love with others. Double blessing!

Talk to an adult about some ways you can help people in need. Make a list and then pick one you like. As you go about your day, make sure to thank God for your food, clothes, bed, and home.

*I urge you to live a life worthy of the calling you
have received. Be completely humble and gentle; be
patient, bearing with one another in love.*
EPHESIANS 4:1-2

FRIENDSHIPS CAN BE TRICKY. ONE FRIEND MIGHT GET mad at another. Someone might say something mean about someone else. A friend you usually eat lunch with might start eating lunch with another group. What are you supposed to do? Each situation will be different, but God gives you instructions on how to handle the drama.

Be humble. Don't worry about being important, noticed, or right all the time. Make sure to listen to others and consider their viewpoints. **Be gentle.** Take a breath before you shout out a comeback, a defense, an insult, or point the blame. **Be patient.** Hurt feelings need time to heal. Arguments take time to work out. Trust that God is at work in all the in-between moments. **Love.** Show love to the friend who is hurt and the friend who supposedly hurt them. Chances are you don't know everything that person is going through. By letting everyone know you care, they'll usually be able to find the courage and kindness to resolve the problems.

Make some word art out of the following words: "Humble," "Patient," "Gentle," and "Love." Or search their definitions in the dictionary. As you doodle or google, ask God to help you be humble, patient, gentle, and loving with your friends and your frenemies.

DAY 88

> *Sow your seed in the morning, and at evening let your hands*
> *not be idle, for you do not know which will succeed, whether*
> *this or that, or whether both will do equally well.*
>
> ECCLESIASTES 11:6

SO MANY CHOICES! YOU'VE SEEN COUNTLESS FLYERS, texts, and emails from school about different clubs, events, teams, and sports. Your church might offer mission trips, retreats, festivals, and game nights. Your community might host parades, contests, and races. You certainly don't have time to try all these things, but you do have opportunities to try new things.

If your teacher announces an essay contest about a topic that interests you, why not write down your thoughts? If there's a pie-baking competition for the Fourth of July festivities and you like to bake, this is your chance to try a pie. Always wanted to play guitar? Check out a YouTube video labeled "Free Beginner Guitar Lesson." Never played soccer before? Why not sign up with some friends for the rec league at the local park? God has loaded you with abilities, some of which you haven't even discovered yet. Try something new today that interests you and see what you can do!

What are some things you've never done before but would like to try? Write them down and talk to God about which ones He might like you to check out. Circle one you can attempt this month. Invite a friend to join you.

*See what great love the Father has lavished on us, that we
should be called children of God! And that is what we are!*

1 JOHN 3:1

LAVISH. IT MEANS TO GIVE GENEROUSLY OR EXTRAVA-
gant quantities of. Like your little cousin might lavish glue on her
crafts, putting so much on that it oozes stickiness everywhere. Or
you might lavish frosting on the cookies you decorate, so every bite
has a thick, creamy layer. Or maybe your neighbor lavishes their
home with so many Christmas lights you can see them twinkling
way down at the other end of the street.

John, who called himself "the disciple Jesus loved," knew all
about Jesus and His love and said that Jesus lavishes His love on
you. Jesus gives you His love generously in crazy, huge, extravagant
amounts. Jesus' love for you is everywhere, overflows, and can be
seen a mile away. Some people in your life might hold back their
love or seem like they love you one day but not the next. With some
people it's just hard to know how they feel. But not Jesus. His love
for you is abundant, constant, and lavish. It will never run out. No
matter how anyone else treats you, no matter how you feel about
yourself, Jesus loves you. Lavishly.

*Thank You, Jesus for loving me so much, in ways I can't even
understand or imagine. Thank You for loving me even when I
mess up, get frustrated with myself, or when other people make me
feel unloved. Help me feel and understand Your lavish love. Amen.*

> *I keep my eyes always on the LORD. With him at*
> *my right hand, I will not be shaken.*
>
> PSALM 16:8

HAVE YOU EVER SHAKEN UP A SODA AND THEN OPENED the lid? What happened? Foam and fizz probably exploded everywhere!

That same thing can happen when you allow yourself to get shaken up. When your coach criticizes you, your parents ask you to clean up your sibling's mess, you're running late, can't find your key, or get blamed for something you didn't do, how do you handle it? Do you freak out and let your anger or emotions explode everywhere? Or do you keep your eyes on Jesus?

When you look to Jesus, He will give you peace you can't find on your own. He will help you catch your breath and calm down. He loves you no matter what your coach says, what your sibling does, whether you're on time or not, where you left your keys, and no matter whose fault it was. The next time you find yourself about to explode, take a deep breath and ask Jesus to help you not get shaken up.

Dear Jesus, _____ shakes me up sometimes. Could You please calm me when I face this person or thing? I'd really love Your peace to replace my emotions when they get out of control. Thank You. Amen.

Dear friend, do not imitate what is evil but what is good.
Anyone who does what is good is from God.

3 JOHN 1:11

THERE IS ALWAYS "THAT KID" IN CLASS, ON THE TEAM, OR IN THE group. They cut others down and everyone laughs. They post nastygrams on social media, and everyone likes them. They show up in an offensive T-shirt and for some reason everyone thinks it's so cool, even though it's clearly not. That person seems like they have something special, and they'll be the first one to tell you about it.

You can't figure out why everyone is so charmed by them. But they are. Be careful here.

Even if that kid gets all the attention, it is not the kind of focus you want. When you stop to think about who you truly want to be, I'm guessing it's not nasty, snarky, or self-important. That person is not worth imitating or hanging around. Remember, God sees you as His masterpiece. He made you wonderfully to inspire awe. You don't have to earn attention or approval at anyone's expense. You don't ever need to be like anyone else. You are already prized by the King of kings.

List some things you know God created you to be. Stuck? Here are some ideas—clever, good listener, curious, full of energy. Focus on being these things today. When you're tempted to imitate someone else, go back to your list and remember all the great things God made you to be.

DAY 92

He says, "Be still, and know that I am God."

PSALM 46:10

HURRY UP. GET MOVING. DO YOU HAVE EVERYTHING? What time is it? Hop in the car. The bus will be here any minute. We're going to be late!

Does this sound like your life at all? There's homework, activities, chores, friends, family, and maybe a job. You might be involved in church, sports, volunteering, scouts, or dance. The list goes on and on and your calendar gets fuller and fuller.

But God says, "Be still."

When was the last time you were completely still? Sleeping doesn't count. When you're still, you can exhale some of the stress. Your swirling thoughts can start to unwind. When you're still, you have a chance to talk to God and, even better, hear Him talking to you. When you're still, great ideas come to you, you can think through issues and problems, you can sort through your emotions, and you can catch your breath.

Before you go off in another direction, take a moment to be still.

Find a quiet spot. Turn off your phone. Put down your pen. Close your eyes. Thank God for being so amazing. Sit in silence for a few mindful minutes thanking God for His peace and love.

"For everyone who asks receives; the one who seeks finds;
and to the one who knocks, the door will be opened."

MATTHEW 7:8

HAVE YOU READ THE STORIES LIKE ALADDIN, WHERE SOMEONE discovers a genie and is granted three wishes?

What if you had three wishes? What would they be? Real wishes. Not just "I wish it would stop raining," or "I wish I didn't have any homework." You don't want to waste your wish. Eventually it will stop raining. And you probably need to do your homework, so you'll have the knowledge or persistence necessary to chase the dreams God has put in your heart.

Jesus says if we ask Him, if we look for Him, if we knock on His door, He will answer us and show us what we're looking for. How awesome is that? The only catch? You have to ask, look, and knock. Have you asked Jesus through prayer to help make your hopes come true? Have you looked in Scripture for answers to your questions? Have you knocked by stepping forward and believing God can help? Why not start now?

Write down three wishes. Take some time to really think through them. Ask Jesus for help in making these wishes come true. Ask Him what you can do. It might mean researching, practicing, or babysitting to save money. Keep asking and listening. God will unlock the door for you to the dreams He's planted in your heart.

The LORD God said, "It is not good for the man to be
alone. I will make a helper suitable for him."

GENESIS 2:18

SOMETIMES YOU NEED YOUR SPACE. BUT THAT CAN'T BE
all the time. God never wanted humans to be alone. In fact, when
God was creating the world, He declared how everything that He'd
created was good—land and sea, sun and stars, fish and birds. But
the first thing that God said wasn't good was for the human He'd
created, Adam, to be alone. When God saw that it was bad for a person to be alone, He immediately created a companion for Adam.
Her name was Eve.

Alone time can be good, healing even. But being alone for
extended periods of time is not good for your emotional health.
Being around others helps you understand yourself, the world, and
God better. Friends and family can help you solve problems, comfort you when you're sad, help you study for a test, laugh at your
jokes, pray for you, and join you in a game of cards or a dance party.
How wonderful that God created you to be with others. Find time
to intentionally connect with your favorite humans today.

Dear God, thank You for knowing I shouldn't be alone and for
creating other people for me to connect with. On days I'd rather
keep to myself, please give me the courage to reach out to others.
Thank You for being with me always. Amen.

Gracious words are a honeycomb, sweet to
the soul and healing to the bones.
PROVERBS 16:24

BULLYING USUALLY BEGINS WITH ONE PERSON USING unkind words about someone else. The words might seem harmless. They might sound normal. Just a comment, like "Let's sit over here," except *here* means away from a specific person. It might be a general statement about how you can't believe some people have never heard of that band. But in all those instances somebody is intentionally excluding someone else. Somebody is implying they are better than someone else. Those words are powerful.

Unkind words are powerful, but kind words are just as powerful. A kind word can change everything. Saying "Let's sit with these people," or "You don't need to whisper, everyone can hear," or "I think everybody listens to and likes different music" are all quick phrases that totally change the mood from possibly hurting someone's feelings to possibly making them feel better.

Be mindful of your words today. Choose to speak kind, healing, life-giving words. To others and to yourself.

Look up the definition and synonyms for the word "include." Talk to God about ways you can use kind words today to make others feel included. Thank God for always including you in His love, His grace, and His protection.

*"And I myself will be a wall of fire around it," declares
the LORD, "and I will be its glory within."*
ZECHARIAH 2:5

A LOT OF DIFFERENT THINGS ARE GOING TO COME YOUR
way today. Are you ready?

People might compliment you, ask you to do something,
expect you to have done things, and criticize something you've
done. You will soar, and you will stumble. You will have a moment
when you wish you had more, and you will have a moment you are
so thankful you have what you have.

Through each and every one of these instances, God is with
you. He will protect you like armor, like a wall of fire, from insults
and injuries. He will motivate you from within to keep going and
stay true to who He made you to be. God keeps you safe from the
outside and builds you up from the inside. No matter what comes
your way, God has you covered.

Draw a picture, write a poem or song, or visualize how God covers
you like bubble wrap, keeping you safe from harm, and how He
fills you like your favorite meal, giving you energy and strength.
As you create, ask God to help you realize how fully He is with you
in all you do.

Pile your troubles on God's shoulders—he'll
carry your load, he'll help you out.
PSALM 55:22 MSG

EVERYONE HAS THINGS THEY'RE WORRIED ABOUT. YOU might be worried about a conversation you need to have, a decision you need to make, a friend who is struggling, something you need to accomplish, how you'll do on a test or tryout, or a relative who is sick.

But God tells us we can pile our troubles on Him, that He'll carry the load for us. This feels hard to believe sometimes. But it's true. God loves you so much that He doesn't want you to worry. Just like you don't want your friend to struggle or your relative to be sick. Sure, you still live in this world and have to take the tests or have the hard conversations or make the decision, but you don't have to do those things alone. You don't have to stress out about how things will turn out, because God will help you.

Create a "worry box." Find a small cardboard box and some paper. Every time you get stressed or worried this week, write down your concern and put it in the box. As you do, tell God you don't want this worry anymore. You are handing it over to Him.

Dear God, thank You so much for saying You'll help, for offering to take my troubles from me. Please help me turn them over to You and accept the help you give. Amen.

This is the day that the LORD has made;
let us rejoice and be glad in it.

PSALM 118:24 ESV

TODAY. THIS DAY THAT YOU'RE LIVING? IT'S PACKED WITH potential and possibilities! God has so much in store for you. Today you might meet a new friend, learn a new skill, make a breakthrough, take a step forward, discover a new place, or realize how good you are at something you'd never even tried before. Today might be the day you experience healing or reconciliation or recovery.

Today you might hear your new favorite song, feel the sun warm on your face, or find a caterpillar and let its fuzzy feet tickle the palm of your hand. Maybe you'll write a vulnerable poem that expresses your feelings perfectly or bake the most delicious blueberry muffins.

However this day starts, you get to choose to let it happen to you, or to live it fully, to rejoice and be glad in it. Keep your ears, eyes, and heart open to what God has in store, to the opportunities waiting for you just around the corner, and then have a blast enjoying this day God made.

Dear God, thank You for this day and all its possibilities. Help me to live fully and rejoice in this life You give me. Amen.

Come near to God and he will come near to you.
JAMES 4:8

YOU KNOW WHERE TO FIND YOUR FRIENDS. YOU MIGHT see them at school, practice, or your favorite park. You know where to find your family—you most likely live under the same roof! If you want to find your dog, all you have to do is call for her, and she'll come running. But how do you find God?

The cool thing about God is He's everywhere. Attending church, going to youth group, listening to worship music, and reading your Bible are awesome places to find God. But just like you can find your friends other places than the halls of school, you can find God other places too. You can find reminders of Him everywhere you go. You can consider God's warmth as you cozy up to a bonfire, marvel at His majesty as you gaze at the glow of the moon, be reminded of His constancy in the beat of your heart or of your favorite song, and sense how much He loves you when you hug a loved one.

All you have to do is look for God, talk to Him, thank Him for His awesomeness, and God will be there. Every time.

Even though this book is coming to an end, God's love for you will never end. He is everywhere, and He is always with you. Make a list of all the places you'll go tomorrow. Write down how you might find God there. Thank God for being everywhere!

Being confident of this, that he who began a good work in you
will carry it on to completion until the day of Christ Jesus.

PHILIPPIANS 1:6

YOU HAVE BEEN DOING A GOOD WORK.

Going through this devotional has been so good for your soul. You've learned so much about God and His love for you. You've learned all kinds of tricks to take care of your mental health and why that matters. God made you and has so much in store for you. You've learned to practice gratitude, get outside, be still, enjoy the company of others, embrace who God created you to be, get moving, be mindful, practice self-care, pray, rest, be gentle with yourself, be creative, stand up for what's right, and help others.

And now that you're on the last page, it doesn't mean all this goodness is over. In fact, it's just beginning. When God plants seeds, He always grows amazing things from them. When He starts good work, He always brings it to completion. You should be so proud of yourself for how far you've come and so excited for how God is going to continue to grow you.

Dear Jesus, thank You for being so loving, so powerful, and for always fighting for me and caring for me. Please help me remember all I learned about talking to You, reading the Bible, and trusting You. Please continue to grow my faith and my relationship with You. Amen.

NOTES

1. Kirsten Weir, "Nurtured by Nature," *American Psychological Association* 51, no. 3 (April 2020): 50, https://www.apa.org/monitor/2020/04/nurtured-nature.

2. Caroline Leaf, *Switch on Your Brain: The Key to Peak Happiness, Thinking, and Health* (Baker Books, 2013), 24.

3. Sarah Garone, "8 Physical and Mental Health Benefits of Silence, Plus How to Get More of It," Healthline, September 23, 2021, https://www.healthline.com/health/mind-body/physical-and-mental-health-benefits-of-silence.

4. Sara Lindberg, "8 Benefits of Dance," Healthline, May 10, 2019, https://www.healthline.com/health/fitness-exercise/benefits-of-dance.

5. Stephen G. Post, "How Helping Others Helps You," Mental Health America, accessed May 30, 2022, https://www.mhanational.org/help-others.

6. Craig T. Lee, "Screen Zombies: Average Person Will Spend 44 YEARS Looking at Digital Devices — And That's Before COVID!", Study Find, December 26, 2020, https://www.studyfinds.org/

screen-zombies-average-person-spends-44-years-looking-at-devices.

7. Kim Kilmas, "The Meaning and History of SOS," On All Bands, February 27, 2020, https://www.onallbands.com/the-meaning-and-history-of-sos/

8. Ben Church and Jill Martin, "Simone Biles Withdraws from All-Around Final at Tokyo 2020 to Focus on Mental Health," CNN, July 28, 2021, https://www.cnn.com/2021/07/28/sport/simone-biles-gymnastics-tokyo-2020-mental-health-spt-intl/index.html.

9. Rhett Power, "Day of Rest: 12 Scientific Reasons it Works," INC., January 1, 2017, https://www.inc.com/rhett-power/a-day-of-rest-12-scientific-reasons-it-works.html.

NOTES

NOTES

NOTES

NOTES

NOTES

NOTES

NOTES

....

....

....

....

....

....

....

....

....

....

....

....

....

....

NOTES

....
....
....
....
....
....
....
....
....
....
....
....
....
....

NOTES

....
....
....
....
....
....
....
....
....
....
....
....
....
....

NOTES

NOTES

NOTES

NOTES

NOTES

NOTES

....

....

....

....

....

....

....

....

....

....

....

....

....

....

NOTES

....

....

....

....

....

....

....

....

....

....

....

....

....

....

NOTES

NOTES

From the Publisher

GREAT BOOKS

ARE EVEN BETTER WHEN THEY'RE SHARED!

Help other readers find this one:

- Post a review at your favorite online bookseller

- Post a picture on a social media account and share why you enjoyed it

- Send a note to a friend who would also love it—or better yet, give them a copy

Thanks for reading!

ABOUT THE AUTHOR

BESTSELLING AUTHOR AND SPEAKER LAURA L. SMITH SPEAKS around the country sharing the love of Christ at conferences and events. She loves Jesus, her prince charming of a husband, their four kids, music, a good book, almond milk mochas, dark chocolate, and travel. Laura lives in the picturesque college town of Oxford, Ohio where you'll find her running the wooded trails, strolling the brick streets, shopping at the Saturday morning farmer's market, or going on a sunset walk with her family. Visit her on Instagram @laurasmithauthor, her website www.laurasmithauthor.com and Facebook @LauraLSmithAuthor.